The Fallacy

The Fallacy

From Bowls to Madness: The Romanticized and often Politicized Argument about the NIL Rights of Intercollegiate Athletes

M. Adkins

The Fallacy

From bowls to madness: The romanticized and often politicized argument about the nil rights of intercollegiate athletes

By Mark Adkins

E Book ISBN: 978-1-7353832-2-4

Paperback ISBN: 978-1-7353832-3-1

Library of Congress Control Number: 2020918891

To my wife and children, Stacy, Silas, and Selah

Table of Contents

PREFACE

INTRODUCTION   2

BACKGROUND   6

GENESIS   8

AMATUERISM   10

UNITED STATES OLYMPIC COMMITTEE (USOC)   12

STUDENT ATHLETE   15

THE FALLACY OF A FREE EDUCATION   18

ATTITUDES AND PERCEPTIONS OF THE AMERICAN
IDEOLOGY   21

CRIMINAL JUSTICE   25

EDUCATION   29

BIG NAMESFOR IT AND BIG NAMES AGAINST
PAYING ATHLETES   34

THE PLAN   38

SCENARIO TWO   45

EPILOGUE   49

THE ATHLETE'S PAGE   **55**

GLOSSARY   58

REFERENCES   68

AUTHOR'S PAGE   80

PREFACE

As I researched the topic, I found that very rich men, the media, certain schools, and the NCAA had been involved in a cover up. For more than a century, the notion of amateurism has kept most student athletes from earning money while competing. This façade has led me to entitle this book, The Fallacy: The Romanticized and often Politicized Argument about the NIL Rights of Intercollegiate Athletes. This book is about the rights of intercollegiate athletics and the money they should and will be making for their talent and sport performances. This book is also about bringing to light to the social connectivity of injustice, inequity, and the divide of race and class. If everything was equal in this world, would we need laws, such as, Title VI, Title IX, or laws that prohibit certain groups rights, such as, the exclusion act, the Pig, and Jim Crow laws of the south. The idea of the American dream was not meant for all. It was only meant for a few who make up the status quo and their chosen microcosm of minorities. Carter Woodson, in his text, The Mis-Education of the Negro, eloquently penned an evaluative observation of minorities who take offense to uplifting other minorities out of the current financial and societal class system of America. He stated that this little minority microcosm would just about do anything to keep their status even advocate for laws to keep other minority groups subservient to others. This type of ignorance has me pondering the words of W.E.B. Dubois, "Either America will destroy ignorance or ignorance will destroy America."

___ M. Adkins

*"In battle, if you make your opponent flinch
you have already won."*

~ Miyamoto Musashi

INTRODUCTION

Ed O'Bannon, a member of the 1995 National Champion UCLA Bruins, decided to take the NCAA to court after viewing himself and other college legends of the past in a video game that was sponsored by the NCAA. After many years away from the game and college, the NCAA was still able to make money off his Name, Image, and Likeness. He felt this was not right so he courageously took on the NCAA and won. His case was the catalyst for Senate Bill 206 and other proposed bills around the country (O'Bannon, 2018). This is where our story begins...

When we were young our mothers, fathers, and often times grandparents would teach us right from wrong. They would use different mediums to do this. Some would use their words by stating, "don't do this because of that." Others use religious texts, fables, and fairytales to get the job done. History reminds us, as a people, we should strive to do right but something always seems to get in the way of this thought process; race, class, and profits. Some of the legendary battles of good versus evil have been Colin Kaepernick versus the NFL, Ed O'Bannon versus the NCAA, and Cinderella. Yes! I said Cinderella.

In the story Cinderella, the evil step sisters treat Cinderella as an indentured servant although they were supposed to be sisters. They would do anything and everything to make her feel as if she was second class and beneath them even though it was her father who married their mother (Grimm et al, 2014). Cinderella is a story that can be compared to the plight of the big-time college sport student athlete. The evil step mother and step sisters are represented by the NCAA and their agents. The NCAA has been relentless in their pursuit of doing anything and everything to keep the student athletes of big-time college sports (Basketball and Football), their cash cow, indentured and in a position of servitude. Most of these athletes tend to be African-American. Nancy Skinner and Steven Bradford, the two senators who sponsored the bill that would help change the student athlete's indentured status, would be the fairy Godparents. Senate Bill 206 represents the glass slipper. Governor Gavin Newsom, symbolizes the prince who signed SB 206. The signing of SB 206 helps all student athletes, I might add. With the signing of SB 206 or placing the slipper in a position to be worn comes the political, social, and racial divide stemming from the idea of compensating big-time college sports student athletes based upon their NIL rights.

The melting pot of humanity has never been a pot of assimilation as it relates to equity. It has always been radicalized due to a desire for hegemonic dominance. Through the means of strategic planning, countries have always used a type of strategy to evoke war, as well as, to win wars. Men seeking hegemonic dominance have instigated revolutions, civil wars, and sought independence when the epiphany of hegemony and profits arrived in their brains. The recipe for these calculated power grabs can be found in the constructs of propaganda and hysteria. The dictionary describes propaganda as information, rumors, etc., deliberately spread widely to help or harm a person, group, movement, institution, and or nation. The dictionary depicts hysteria as uncontrollable outbursts often characterized by irrationality.

The Salem witch trials is a historical illustration on how propaganda and hysteria work collaboratively. Now, if we formulated an example on how this concept permeates through the fabric of big-time college sports the vignette would be voiced this way. For instance, amateurism has always been about higher, braver, faster, the Olympic motto. It's never been about money. If you start paying athletes, collegiate sport is doomed. It would cause us to lose interest and stop watching intercollegiate sport. It would rob the athlete, as well as, the fans of athletic performances that were actualized just for the sheer challenge of competing on an aesthetical, figurative, and symbolic level. We should start a protest across university and college campuses, in the media, as well as in communities stating they shouldn't get paid. Those college athletes already get paid. They receive a college education for free. That's payment enough. Right!

The above vignette displays the type of rhetoric that sport organizations pedal and have continued to push to keep the collegiate bread winners of sport subservient, broke, injured, and sometimes replaced. For example, the case of James Wiseman of the University of Memphis. James Wiseman is a 7-foot one, African American college basketball player who will be a top draft pick in the 2020 NBA draft. Penny Hardaway, NBA hall of famer, now the coach of Memphis gave Wiseman's family $11,500 to move to Memphis. The NCAA knew about the money and had deemed him eligible for the 2019-2020 season. Then in one wave of the hand deemed him ineligible.

In another instance, Joe Burrow, LSU's Quarterback, stated on a podcast that he wasn't a student athlete anymore and admitted that after the National Championship game, Odell Beckham Jr. was handing out real money to the LSU players after their victory over Clemson. Many onlookers were elated that Odell Beckham's actions seemed to heckle the NCAA and their rules of amateurism. It is somewhat duplicitous that everyone can earn money off the backs of student athletes except the ones doing all the work, the student athletes themselves. While big businesses, post-secondary schools, administrators, and their coaches feed off lucrative TV contracts, advertisements, and product endorsements to get filthy rich. In this situation the NCAA is probably powerless. Coaches, fans, commenters, members of Congress and etc., are starting to realize this is an unfair and an inhumane practice (McCann, 2020).

After vehemently refuting California's Senate Bill 206, the National Collegiate Athletic Association NCAA had a stunning reversal of their previous stance on the fair pay to play declaration. This unexpected revelation will pave the way for all student athletes to have the same rights as any other student on post-secondary institution campuses. This will allow them, through their own creative aptitude or physical prowess, to earn money stemming from their ability or talents.

No matter what the NCAA proposes it will definitely be more restrictive than California's SB 206. Mark Emmert, the NCAA President, has communicated that he would like to work with congress to create a set of protocols that would allow college athletes in each state opportunities to earn monetary assets off their name, image, and likeness. To ensure this action is in fact the real plan, Ramogi Huma, founder of National Collegiate Player Association NCPA, has been speaking to congress as well helping various states draft legislation to put into law to protect the athletes NIL rights going forward (Murphy, 2020).

In January 2023, student athletes will be able to receive earnings from corporations for the use of their name, image, and or likeness NIL. Post-secondary institutions will have to change a certain amount of their campaigns and initiatives and find some way to create a sense of fairness, marketability, and profitability away from the name, image, and likeness of the student athlete. These changes are likely to come in the form of strategic management.

*"There is a price to pay for speaking the truth.
There is a bigger price for living a lie."*

~ Dr. Cornel West

BACKGROUND

It is hard to believe the pay to play concept has been around for 68 years. When the NCAA elected for a grant-in-aid system, it was characterized as a pay to play scheme (Byers, 1995). It is even harder to fathom that the idea of the student athlete emerged out of the fact the NCAA didn't want to pay worker's compensation (Loretta8, 2014). With these two revelations, it is almost unconscionable that the NCAA's longest serving executive director, Walter Byers, would utter over 35 years ago the following; "The structure we have in place as a means of controlling the activities of recruiting and financial aid must go through a dramatic change. Is there anything that can keep big-time college athletics operating within the rules? That's the real question. I'm gradually coming to the conclusion that there has to be a major rearrangement on the part of the institutions of higher learning as to what they want to do with their athletic programs .... It's the Me Generation. It's mine and I want it now. Well, why not? I think back in time. It used to be that a rich alumnus could get a needy kid out of a Gary, Indiana steel mill and send him to Yale. Then the NCAA came along with a bunch of rules and said, 'You can't do that.' An alumnus can't send a kid to school to play athletics? But is it wrong for the donor to give the boy the money? No, I'm feeling that it's only the colleges with the rules that say it's wrong. The coaches don't think it's so wrong anymore. The public doesn't think it's so wrong (McCallum, 1984)."

Now back to the future, at least for the moment, the NCAA has seemed to have folded its current hand to repudiate California's Senate Bill 206, the Fair Pay to Play Act, and have decreed an edict to post-secondary intercollegiate sport divisions to lay out a plan to allow companies, corporations, and entities to pay intercollegiate student athletes for the use of their name, image, and likeness NIL by January 2021 (Brooks, 2019). When and if this happens, student athletes will have the same privileges and freedoms as other students to capitalize monetarily from their skills, abilities, and talents, while preserving the due diligence of the collegiate experience beyond the state of California. The 1,117 participating institutions will surely undergo substantial changes to their institutional outcomes, objectives, initiatives, and campaigns, resulting from outside organizations vying to pay student athletes for the use of their name, image, and likeness NIL.

THE FALLACY

"Let there be light"; and there was light.

~ Higher power

GENESIS

Toward the second half of the 19th Century, the culture of the United States (U.S.) was still Victorian. The Victorian culture accentuated its influence around the concept of the Muscular Christian. It was a notion that synthesized physical feats and religious allegiance. Intercollegiate football seemed to be the binding glue to this merger. American Intercollegiate football is a cross between two sports, World Football or Soccer and Rugby. The first college football game was played between Rutgers and Princeton in 1869. Since that momentous day, football has undergone many instrumental innovations. The man responsible for most of these revisions was Walter Camp, known as the father of American football. He was responsible for overhauling the rules of the game. He first reduced the size of the team from 15 to 11. He rid football of the rugby scrum where players were huddled around each other, and then the referee tosses the ball into the anxious group of players to gain ball possession. Camp revolutionized other ideas as well, such as, the kick-off, line scrimmage, and downs. These refinements led to more manageable games and gave way to scripted plays and tactical strategies.

The media of the time had a love hate relationship with intercollegiate football. Some were devoted to it, due to the fact that it filled a void after the baseball season had ended. The deans of the post-secondary institutions began to notice that journalists were dedicated and committed to football. The media print meant public exposure which translated into financial investment by the alumni's, business entities, and the general public. In addition, a side effect caused by intercollegiate football was the decrease of student physical conflicts on campus and an increase in a common focus towards a goal. This common focus, termed school spirit, flowed throughout the entire campus. However, some journalists did not share the same affinity for the sport. They called it a Death Harvest since it was played in the Fall and due to its roughness. Others reported that "Football Fills More Coffins", due to the untimely deaths of college players. Teddy Roosevelt, the president during this time often praised the roughness of football. In 1890, President Roosevelt at a banquet stated, "What matters a few broken bones to the glories of intercollegiate sport?" President Roosevelt's attitude changed when Ted Roosevelt Jr. entered Harvard in 1905. During the Yale Harvard freshmen match up, Ted Roosevelt Jr. suffered a broken nose. He assured his presidential father he was only bruised but otherwise okay. The injury suffered by Ted Roosevelt Jr. and the media outcry calling on President Roosevelt to bring forth an end to football put him in a precarious predicament (Beschloss, 2014). For example, through the provocation of an open letter, the Chicago Tribune elicited action from Theodore Roosevelt by highlighting the fact that forty-five players had been killed between 1901 and 1905. So in turn, Roosevelt was prompted to request a meeting between Bill Reid (Harvard's Football coach), Walter Camp (Yale's football coach), and Arthur Hillenbrand (Princeton's football coach).The dialogue and deliberation bore fruit of a gentleman's agreement, and a handshake insisting on certain rules related to roughness, holding, and treachery be changed.

After a year of waiting in 1906, thirty-six schools enacted the Intercollegiate Athletic Association IAA as its governing body. In 1910, the IAA changed its name to the National Collegiate Athletic Association NCAA. Before the NCAA, post-secondary institutions also would engage in a type of open enrollment toward football players that showed a high level of ability in regard to the game including speed, agility, and strength. These players seemed to materialize at the beginning of the season and vanished by the last game. They were all retained to ensure a good winning season for the institutions and were paid substantial salaries.

"Don't let them pull the wool over your eyes."

~ Unknow author

AMATUERISM

The NCAA, modern texts and references, as well as, society cling to the belief that the concept of amateur athletics fell from the hands of the Greeks only to be used by the modern world in the way they chose to portray it. It is funny to contemplate that the ancient Greeks did not even have a word for the term amateur (Mahaffy, 1879). The term amateur evolved from the word amator, which means lover in Latin. So, someone could deduce that an amateur is someone looking for love. It first appeared in the English language in 1786 (Jennings, 2016). The NCAA defines the phrase amateur status, as it relates to athletics, as following; an individual will not be eligible for intercollegiate competition in a particular sport if the individual uses his or her athletics skill in any way for pay or accepts a promise of pay, signs a contract, or has a commitment of any kind to play professional athletics. Also, an individual will not be eligible for intercollegiate competition if an individual receives a salary or any type of financial assistance from a professional sport agency, unless permitted by the NCAA. In addition, eligibility will be lost if an individual competes on any professional athletic team unless permitted. Furthermore, an individual will forfeit their eligibility if they enter into a professional draft and enter into an agreement with an agent (NCAA, 2018). However, the term athlete in ancient Greek means competitor for a prize (Mahaffy, 1879). So, putting the two words together makes them somewhat oxymoronic.

Regarding amateurism, Myles Brand, executive director of NCAA from 2002-2009, sold the collegiate model to the universities and the general public by insisting that athletics had an educational benefit which was fundamentally essential for its presence and practice on post-secondary campuses. He did this without addressing the rampant commercialized environment that has always thrived and plagued collegiate athletics. Brand had justified and further clarified his position on commercialism in collegiate sports in his 2006 state of the association address:

"Athletics, like the university as a whole, seeks to maximize revenue. In respect, it has an obligation to conduct its revenues-generating activities in a productive and sound business-like manner... That is on the revenue side, in input, athletics, like the university itself, must follow the best business practice." The conundrum that emerged from this type of business earnings, seemingly produced by his own collegiate model refuted the bylaws of the NCAA. For instance, athletes weren't supposed to endorse products even if they themselves did not receive payment. The NCAA looks at this action as exploitation. Case in point, the NCAA in 2003 ventured into an endorsement deal with Pontiac. Fans were able to vote on their favorite NCAA intercollegiate sport moment. These sport moments included names, images, and likenesses of athletes. The schools and the NCAA profited greatly from Pontiac's sponsorship. The only individuals that did not profit was the athletes, hence exploitation (Nocera & Strauss, 2018).

THE FALLACY

"Something is always better than nothing."

~ Unknown

UNITED STATES OLYMPIC COMMITTEE (USOC)

In his speech, at the inaugural Olympic opening ceremonies, Baron Pierre de Coubertin uttered these words "Keep away the opportunities that are advanced by profit driven individuals whose only dream is to use someone else's muscle either to build upon his own political fortune or to make his own business prosper." Baron de Coubertin's proved to be somewhat of a clairvoyant, when he issued this cautionary rebuke to individuals who wanted to corrupt the games by commercializing them (Barney et al, (2002 pg. 26). As Dorothy from the Wizard Oz once said, "We're a long way from Kansas, Toto." In the above statement given by Baron de Coubertin, the idea of the Olympic Games representing something higher, greater, and faster, in an ideological sense has gone by the wayside. From the fiasco with the Helms Company to the Jim Thorpe experiment, the Olympics Games are now immersed in commercialism. Amateurism, preserving rights, and the status of the student athletes were once championed by the NCAA and the USOC, but has begun to blur. In 2001, the NCAA initiated a rule change that sanctioned the USOC's Operation Gold program. The United States Olympic Committee's Operation Gold is a program designed to reward Olympics athletes who achieve medals during the Olympics. Gold medalists could earn $25,000 for a gold, $15,000 for a silver, and $10,000 for a bronze. In the years when the Olympics are actually taking place, these athletes can receive multiple monetary awards. For example, U.S. swimmer Katie Ledecky of Stanford University and Joseph Schooling of the University of Texas each earned six figures for their Olympic efforts, while still retaining their amateur status. It is interesting that the NCAA can deny the bread winners of intercollegiate sports, such as, basketball and football players, from earning money during their college careers, but allow others to profit financially. In years past, Mark Spitz took one photo after he had won seven Gold Medals and was declared a professional. Michael Phelps, used his agent to solicit a rule change to keep his amateur status until he decided to turn professional (Hodler, 2018).

Furthermore, in June of 2019, the International Olympic Committee (IOC) voted on several reforms. One of which is the changing of rule 40 (Sport Business, 2019). Rule 40 is a statute introduced and ratified in 1991 for the aspiration of preserving international marketing and sponsorship competition related to the Olympic games (Team USA, 2020). Before this modification, Rule 40 prevented all Olympic or Paralympic athletes from using their name, image, and likeness for financial benefit. Rule 40 only allowed the IOC approved sponsors to earn monetary capital related to the games. Now, the United States Olympic and Paralympic Committee USOPC are allowing athletes to openly thank sponsors through the media for a monetary benefit. Those same sponsors can give complementary messages, as well as, produce advertisements. Han Xiao, the chairman of the USOPC athletes' advisory council, states, "This guidance enables athletes' opportunities in an entirely new way and is a sign of great progress (Wharton, 2019)." Although this modification to rule 40 allows athletes to be compensated for their NIL rights there are some limitations, such as, the phrases Tokyo 2020, Team USA, and Olympic imagery. Also, athletes can not endorse products that are not officially promoted by the USOPC with phrases like "Your product is the best (Mather, 2019)."

Consequently, due to the world-wide public safety crisis amid the coronavirus pandemic, Shinzo Abe, Prime Minister of Japan, and Thomas Bach, the president of the International Olympic Committee (IOC), reached an accord suspending the Tokyo Olympics until July of 2021, (Ramsay, 2020). Although this may be the official plan that the Japanese government has expressed, Kentaro Iwata, a professor of infectious disease, has come forward in disagreement with the 15-month postponement. He states, "I don't think the Olympics is likely to be held next year. Holding the Olympics needs two conditions: one, controlling COVID-19 in Japan, and controlling COVID-19 everywhere." Zach Binney, an American epidemiologist at Emory University, expressed a similar sentiment by stating, "When we talk about bringing sports back, with packed stadiums, I really think that is something we are going to have to wait for a vaccine to be able to do (Aljazeera, 2020)." In addition to these comments, Dr. Anthony Fauci the director of the National Institute of Allergy and Infectious Diseases, stated this; "Safety, for the players and for the fans, trumps everything. If you can't guarantee safety, then unfortunately you're going to have to bite the bullet and say, we may have to go without this sport for this season." He further concluded, "If we let our desire to prematurely get back to normal, we can only get ourselves right back in the same hole we were in a few weeks ago." Unfortunately, we live in a capitalistic society where capitalistic greed trumps the care and well-being of people's lives (Wagner & Belson, 2020)

.

"Cheating is not a mistake, it's a decision."

~ Anonymous

STUDENT ATHLETE

Ray Dennison, in 1955 was a member of the Fort Lewis A&M football team. During a kickoff he suffered an injury to his head. The injury to the head eventually killed him two days later. His widow sued for worker's compensation benefits which began the conversation of an athlete's role on campus. Were they college employees with a paid grant in aid scholarship? Or were they students who happened to engage in a sport activity at college. The Supreme Court of Colorado ultimately deciding by stating that the school wasn't in the football business. Although this was seemingly a victory for the school and the NCAA, the process took a toll on Walter Byers. Having the forethought that injuries are sustained in sport, Byers didn't want to be held liable if a judge ever ruled against the NCAA claiming the men's football and basketball were in fact, jobs. Byers changed the four-year grant in aid scholarship to a one-year scholarship that resembled a contract. This move gave the coaches and universities more control over their athletes. Athletes now could be cut from the team for poor play, injury, or anything that the coach or the school deemed unacceptable. The term student athlete was forged to give the impression the athletes are students first, athletes second, and not employees (Nocera & Strauss, 2018).

In another misfortunate incident, Rashidi Wheeler, a twenty-two-year-old strong safety for Northwestern football team died during pre-season conditioning from an exercise induced asthma attack. That day, he had just completed multiple sprinting drills at different distances. When he fell to the ground, Marvin Brown, a teammate helped him to a bench. He stated something was wrong and his veins in his arm didn't look normal. After being placed on the bench, Wheeler looked at another fellow teammate, Kevin Bentley, and said, "K.B. I'm dying." Sean Wieber overheard the same conversation. Within that same hour, Wheeler was dead and practice continued while it was all being filmed. Later, Marvin Brown said that he saw Wheeler take supplements containing ephedrine to control his asthma. In 1997, the NCAA banned the substance but didn't test for the substance until 2002. The Food and Drug Administration began its testing in 2003, due to the risk of stroke and heart attack that came with taking the drug. Dr. Mark Gardner health director at Northwestern at the time burned Wheeler's records, then proceeded to take a permanent leave of absence. Although the Wheeler's got a hefty settlement of $16 million dollar, the NCAA issued no punishment (Nocera & Strauss, 2018) (Lane & Brown, 2016).

Another issue plaguing the student athlete was admissions. In 1948, the Sanity Code was instituted by the NCAA. The Sanity Code was supposedly designed to ensure that all student athletes met all the requirements to enter college. The Sanity Code failed, due to lack of enforcement.

Later in 1965, the NCAA founded the 1.600 rule. The rule was devised and sanctioned to assure that all incoming freshman who participated in athletics and received a grant in aid scholarship earned a 1.600 grade point average on a 4.0 grading scale. This score encompassed the averages of the Scholastic Aptitude Test SAT and the Achievement Test ACT. Still many coaches complained that an athlete who has attained a "C" grade point average (2.0) at an academically rigorous school may achieve an "A" (4.0) average at an institution that had produced less academic rigor. The perceived thought was that any athlete attending a school that had less academic rigor helped the student athlete and the non-athlete and could be construed as a huge advantage in gaining admittance into college. This led to coaches writing the NCAA about ensuring the enforcement of the 1.600 rule. When the NCAA began to investigate claims, the post-secondary institutions later accused the NCAA of over stepping their jurisdiction.

Due to the difference in the caliber of secondary schools pertaining to underserved minorities, in 1969, the National Association of College Admission Counselors endorsed a manifesto recommending increasing the number of African Americans in post-secondary institutions. These students would still have to adhere to the 1.600 rule but the SAT and the ACT were supposedly to be used primarily and strictly for research and diagnostic purposes. This wasn't the case. The two tests were used in the admission process (Byers, 1995).

THE FALLACY

"Ignorance is more costly to any state than education."

~ Booker T. Washington

THE FALLACY OF A FREE EDUCATION

A free ride or free education is a term synonymously used along with athletic scholarship. This term was created by the NCAA and used by universities and colleges to generate a notion that the so-called student athletes were the beneficiaries of alumni boosters or some private philanthropist or endowment. In truth though, you could look upon this student led workforce as a non-paid employees' system, whose work produces billions of dollars each year. Reggie Rivers, a former college player and NFL running back, states "that a federal grant that you do not have to pay back is a free education. A rich uncle could pay your way through college and that would be free, but in the terms of an athletic scholarship, nothing is free when you calculate all the hours involved, such as, meeting, practices, travel, school work, and off-season workouts (Sage, 1998)."

Kareem Adul-Jabbar, a National Basketball League NBA Hall a Famer, in 2014 commented on life as a student athlete more than 50 years ago. At University of California at Los Angeles UCLA, basketball was a 7-day week profession. For instance, he explained, you have practice, home games, and away games where you had to travel from place to place. The school made lots of money from the games and promotions. Although this was true, he stated he was relatively poor. All he could really do was study, practice, and play. The money he did have in his possession came from summer jobs. He also remembered scraping change up in his room after winning a championship and then wondering about all the money the university is pocketing off the victory. Furthermore, he stated that students on academic scholarships are allowed to hold jobs while attending school but student athletes cannot. If an athlete were to sustain an injury where they could not continue in the sport their scholarship could be revoked even if there were medical bills to be paid, due to the injury that occurred on school grounds or on another participating school's grounds (Jabbar, 2018).

In 1995 at University of California Los Angeles, Donnie Edwards a student athlete football player told a radio personality that he didn't have any food in his refrigerator. Although he never asked or never knew at the time, a bag of food was left on his door step. Later it was learned that it was left by a sport agent. This led to him serving an athletic suspension for a year while all along the NCAA was collecting money off the sale of his jersey.

In another instance, Shabazz Napier and the University of Connecticut basketball team in 2014 had just won the NCAA Division I national championship. Thereafter, while talking to reporters he stated he sometimes went to bed hungry, due to the fact he didn't have any money to buy food. According to a 2011-2012 National College Player Association NCPA report, the full ride athletic scholarship left most college student athletes with $3,285 out of pocket bill (NPR, 2014). One can only imagine what the cost out of pocket would be now in 2019.

Conclusion

Since the inaugural football meeting that began the formulation of the NCAA, college sports have been embroiled with capitalism and corruption. For example, Walter Camp, the father of America football, publicly said he would renounce participation for money by stating, "A gentleman never competes for money, directly or indirectly". Privately though he was known for managing a $100,000 slush fund for athletic "tutoring." Although it doesn't seem like much, but if measured in today's money it would be about 2.5 million dollars. He also had a player by the name of James J. Hogan, who lived in a lavish dorm room and paid no fees for his attendance at Yale. He also had cigarette and scorecard businesses on the side while playing football (Goldstein, 2014).

Mark Emmert, the current president of the NCAA, still believes that the reason fans like college sports so much is that they believe the athletes are really students who play for a love of the sport. That statement is absolutely unequivocally naïve since our American society is based on capitalism, and the NCAA has always been commercialized. The president of the NCAA himself earns almost $3 million a year.

Over the years, the NCAA has used the media to create a façade to fabricate history. They constructed a narrative to the extent to serve their purpose and generate wealth. This wealth comes off the backs of the unpaid labored student athletes. Basketball and football, the cash cows of the NCAA, are manipulated through a set of controls that were designed to keep society's hegemonic stratified social system in place. This system generates over $14 billion dollars a year in which the student athletes have not been able to access, due to their amateur status.

"Is there a place for the hopeless sinner
Who has hurt all mankind just to save his own beliefs?"

~ Bob Marley

ATTITUDES and PERCEPTIONS of the AMERICAN IDEOLOGY

The information collected for this book revealed a relationship between paying intercollegiate athletes and the attitudes and perceptions of the American ideology. The relationship, due to its nature, is on same continuum as Critical Race Theory CRT. CRT is a theory that lends itself to open discussions about race and racism in American ideological society (Ladson-Billings,2000; Tate,1997). Racism has been viewed and discussed as a persistent act of assault, either physically, mentally, or socially against persons based on the pigmentation of their skin and other characteristics and attributes (Omi &Winant,1994). White privilege or dominance usually marginalizes minorities voices on issues of race or racism due to social, political, and economic hegemony of the Caucasian society (Feagin, 2000). For these reasons the almost taboo subjects of race and racism in American society very seldomly discuss imperative issues pertaining to those topics. This is due to the difficulty of observing and conversing about racism openly in the context of being systemically oppressed.

Therefore, when it comes to issues of paying student athletes, the country is divided by race. Most Caucasians oppose paying athletes while most African-Americans believe athletes should be paid. Decades of research have uncovered links that show strong differences of opinions between whites and blacks on policies that seem race-neutral, such as paying student athletes.

Sport is a subculture that reflects the value systems of the mainstream society. In 1987, Al Campanis Sr., the Vice

President of the Dodgers, speaking about African American holding managerial jobs in baseball told Ted Koppel of ABC News, "No, I don't believe it's prejudice. I truly believe they may not have some of the necessities to be, let's say, a field manager or perhaps a general manager." "Do you really believe that?", Ted Koppel asks. Al Campanis replied with, "Well, I don't say all of them, but they certainly are short. How many quarterbacks do you have? How many pitchers do you have that are black? ... Why are black men, black people not good swimmers? Because they don't have the buoyancy." Al Campanis was speaking about the cognitive attributes of African Americans and their hardiness for a leadership role in sport. These types of attitudes and perceptions continue to plague sport professionally and intercollegiately. This is why paying college athletes to play, mainly basketball and football college players, is so pivotal in regard to the racial divide (Harris, 2017).

For example, in February 2019, 2,201 American adults were surveyed on the issue of paying college athletes. 55% of the African American adults responded favorably in paying student athletes wages, in comparison to 31% of the Caucasian contingent. Most Caucasian respondents believed a scholarship was adequate compensation for intercollegiate athletes. The survey utilized 1,780 Caucasians and 279 African Americans. The notion of paying college athletes to play has become a conundrum, due to the fact of the consequential ratio of African-Americans to Caucasians in the NCAA's cash cow sports of basketball and football (Burns, 2019).

Another survey was administered with a sample size of 1,013 Americans, using the 2016 Cooperative Congressional Election Study (CCES) of which 164 participants were African-American. The African-Americans were given a list of characterized fictional intercollegiate athletes' names such as, John Jay, John Smith, and Johnson James. While the other non-African American groups received a list of stereotypical names, such as, Lamar Washington, Devonte Walker, and Jamal Adul-Sherif. The respondents were asked to identify the names of the college athletes they recognized. Respondents of the survey were front loaded with the notion of whom might benefit from the policy of pay to play. Some with the notion African Americans would benefit and some with the notion Caucasians would benefit. The results showed that African Americans who were front loaded with the idea that African American student athletes would benefit were 13% more likely to support paying student athletes than when predisposed to Caucasian names by 59.1% to 45.9%. As far as the Caucasian respondents, when they were exposed to fictional characterized Caucasian athletes' names, their results yielded a 16% increase compared to when African American names which resulted in a difference of 31.6% to 15.2 % (Burns, 2019).

Separate but not equal has been central to the American society before and after either the Mendez vs. Westminster or Brown versus the Board of Education cases. Langton Hughes, poet of the Harlem Renaissance era, once wrote, "...America never was America to me, and yet I swear this oath America will be!" Langton Hughes communicated the feelings and attitudes of most the African Americans during his generation which was; why are we (African-American) swearing an oath to protect and defend the republic of America, if it is not reciprocated to us as citizens of America? Although it is hard to change perceptions and attitudes ingrained into a person from their infancy to maturity, one has to wonder why the founders of our constitution wrote in tenets protecting individual and group freedoms, due process rights, and well-being. In the second paragraph of the Declaration of Independence, it states, "We hold these truths to be self-evident, that all men are created equal, that they are endowed by their Creator with certain unalienable Rights, that among these are Life, Liberty, and the pursuit of Happiness".

This begs the questions; What happens if you were never seen as a human being and now suddenly you are? How would your former capturers and or masters see you and treat you? How would they advise their posterity on dealing with you? If you had built a $14 billion dollar industry off the backs of unpaid African American labor would you suddenly starting paying the African American labor because it's the right thing to do?

THE FALLACY

During the Trans-Atlantic Slave Trade, Africans were not recognized as people, but were identified as commodities (Elliot & Hughes, 2019). Joe Feagin, a leading researcher on racial and ethnic relations at Texas A&M, put the blame directly on slavery and the Jim Crow laws when discussing discrepancies in race relations and financial stability of African-Americans. For almost five centuries, African-Americans did not have a sense of equity nor opportunity. Also, African Americans had to withstand the absence of cross generational financial resources (Burns, 2019).

Apart from this, now people are calling for and are forcibly removing statues of men who were involved in the slave trade or who owned slaves. These statues have always stood as a tribute to these individuals and the perseverance of their moral principles. However, these statues also stand as a stark reminder to others of torture and subservience that hegemonic dominance caused. (Echchaibi, 2020).

The hegemonic dominance of one group has infiltrated all facets of American society. It can be found in sport, religion, media, art, and the re-fabrication of history to support a Caucasian narrative. This hegemonic dominance is a reason why there is a racial divide on pay to play in intercollegiate sport. To show that the hegemonic dominance is ingrained into every part of American society the criminal justice department and education will be highlighted in the next chapter.

"Injustice anywhere is a threat to justice everywhere."

~ Martin Luther King Jr.

CRIMINAL JUSTICE

America has a love affair with their police and crime dramas. They love spewing out the idea of protect and serve. This motto has shaped the minds and ideas of the general public. For example, police were asked to protect and serve in Charlottesville, Virginia, where white nationals marched throughout the streets shouting, "Blood and soil" and "You will not replace us," before killing one and leaving 19 injured from fighting with counter-protesters. (Hanna, Hartung, Sayers, & Almasy, 2017). To combat the ideas of the group Black Lives Matter, Congress passed a bill called Blue Lives Matter or the Protect and Serve Bill. The Protect & Serve Act would place anyone who causes bodily harm to an officer of the law to possibly be incarcerated for up to 10 years. The American Civil Liberties Union ACLU, Human Rights Watch, and the NAACP summarized the focus of the act in a conjoined letter. The statement read, "Rather than focusing on policies that address issues of police excessive force, biased policing, and other police practices that have failed these communities, the Protect and Serve Act's aim is to further criminalize". By designing a bill based upon existing statutes of hate crimes, Congress has disparaged the assumption of any type of misconduct by the police against minorities. Therefore, giving the professional apparel of the police and the individuals that wear them almost unlimited jurisdiction, dominion, and command over the communities they are allegedly there to protect and serve (Lennard, 2019). While on the other hand, dark pigmented skinned people are deemed and identified as having a lack of jurisdiction, dominion, and command in their own communities where they make up the majority.

THE FALLACY

In another example, New York Edwin Raymond, a Lieutenant for the New York Police Department NYPD, is suing the department that employs him for discrimination. Constantin Tsachas, the police commander who is at the center of the lawsuit, compelled officers to impose minor violations against African Americans and Latinos, while letting Caucasians and Asian Americans go even if they were in violation. Constantin Tsachas has been recently promoted to deputy inspector. This commander conveyed to the officers under him to think of Asian and Caucasian Americans as soft targets and urged the officers to look for African Americans and Latinos who were jumping turnstiles. Between October 2017 and June 2019, African Americans and Latinos, who make up a little more than half of New York's population were the recipients of 73% more tickets for not paying subway fares. These individuals, the African Americans and Latinos, also made up 90% of the people getting arrested rather than cited with a ticket for minor offenses (Goldstein & Southall, 2019).

In another example, the LAPD investigated more African Americans and Latinos than Caucasians during traffic stops although Caucasians have been found to be more likely to have illegal items in their possession. The analysis established a statistical correlation showing 24% of African American motorists and their passengers across the city are suspected to search and seizures in relation to 16% of Latinos and 5% of Caucasians over a 10-month period. This translates into an African American in a motor vehicle is four times more likely to be pulled over and searched than a person of Caucasian decent. The analysis also showed Latinos were three times more likely to be pulled over than an individual who was Caucasian. Although this is true, Caucasians were searched and found with weapons or other contraband in 20% of the vehicle searches and pat-down searches. This is in comparison to 17% for African Americans and 16% for Latinos. To the community leaders and higher education professionals, these finding damage the already fragile relationship LAPD has with the minority citizens. This reminds some of the 1992 riots sparked by the infamous Rodney King beating (Poston & Chang, 2019).

Although there is no mention of the Los Angeles Sheriff Department LASD in this paper, it does not mean they are clean. A lawyer who was a part of the Knight Ridder investigation into the LASD says "A growing joke in our circles is you never would have had the Rodney King videotape in 1991 if they were sheriff's deputies, they just would have shot him (Nazarvan, 2016)."

Furthermore, similar to Tom Cruise's Minority Report, the LAPD uses a crime predictive software called PredPol. PredPol was created by UCLA professor Jeff Brantingham in partnership with the LAPD to forecast crime in real time over a 12-hour interval (Medium, 2019). The software suite utilizes an algorithm that accesses 10 years of data which covers different types of criminal wrong-doing, particular points of time, and areas in which the infractions took place. Hamid Khan, of the Spying Coalition, states that predictive policing continues to target African Americans and Latinos. The LAPD has announced they will scale back in their use of PredPol (Puente & Chang, 2019).

Aaron Harvey, a resident of San Diego who auspiciously defended himself against gang charges stemming from the use of predictive software, has since become an advocate against state laws pertaining to gangs. He recently stated, that "any time you take out the human perspective or interaction, I don't believe there's any positives." This statement pertains to predictive software used by law enforcement agencies (Winston & Burrington, 2018). In addition, last year, after receiving the results of a federal funded study, the government concluded that facial recognition software is inaccurate. The report noted that the software mis-identifies African-Americans, Native Americans, and Asian-Americans 10 to 100 times more often than European faces, but widespread use amongst the nation's police departments is prevalent (Rattansi, 2020).

Furthermore, in a 2015 audio recording, Michael Bloomberg is heard stating police should be in neighborhoods where minorities live because that's where crime happens. At the Aspen Institute in Colorado in the same year, he was again heard stating 95% of your murders, murders and murder victims, fit one Method of Operation (M.O.). They are all male minorities between the ages of 15 to 25. This is the case in New York and in every other city. As mayor of New York from 2002-2013 he piloted and endorsed the controversial stop-and-frisk program (BBC, 2020). The stop and frisk method encouraged police officers to stop, question, and search citizens who they thought had weapons or drugs based on their own intuition. This approach was deemed a success, due to the falling crime rate. Pro Publica, an independent nonprofit newsroom, discovered that police citizen stops showed an increase from 100,000 in 2002 to 700,000 in 2011. 83% percent of those stops involved African Americans or Latinos. In 2013 the department data proved that 90% of those stops were completely free of any infraction of the law. So, a federal judge ruled that the stop and frisk law was unconstitutional (eji, 2018). Michael Bloomberg, speaking in Brooklyn at a church in November 2019, apologized for his role in promoting the stop and frisk initiative (BBC, 2020). Some advocates point out there may be some long-term psychological effects that stems from multiple police stops. Researchers have expressed concern that frequent police stops can increase stress within an individual and may trigger a PTSD response. Also, the frequency of police stops deter citizens from using public facilities and services. Furthermore, policies similarly to the stop and frisk can induce voter suppression throughout certain neighborhoods (eji, 2018).

Besides these facts, in light of George Floyd's death, who died while being restrained by a police officer's knee on his neck, has ignited communities to call for the defunding of the police. This has motivated Eric Garcetti, the Mayor of Los Angeles to cut a $250 million increase to the police department's budget. Also, Scott Stringer, the New York City Controller, has recommended that the New York Police Department be cut by $1 billion dollars over four years (Siegel, 2020).

*"Until we get equality in education,
we won't have an equal society."*

~ *Supreme Court Justice Sonia Sotomayor*

EDUCATION

In K12 environments, the biggest issue is budgetary funding. State and local governments are embroiled in a racial divide when it comes to funding school districts. EdBuild, a New Jersey research group that focuses on funding for school districts, stated recently that state governments have given more money to school districts having large numbers of minority students, but those same state governments fail to keep pace with school districts deemed Caucasian districts. Districts that have a high number of Caucasian students receive about $23 billion more than school districts that have a large number of minority students attending. The resource gap is largely due to property taxes collected in the more affluent districts. Communities having a substantial number of Caucasians in general tend to be financially stable and are able to pay more taxes to fund schools. In 2016, non-Caucasian districts collected about $54 billion in local tax dollars which translates to about $4,500 per student. In comparison, Caucasian districts with higher wage earners collected $77 billion which translates to $7,000 per student. When looking at a state by state comparison, Arizona illustrated the biggest funding disparity. The districts with a high number of Caucasians received $7,613 more than districts that were classified as minority districts (Meckler, 2019).

In regard to higher education, funding is always an issue, but inclusion, diversity, and or multiculturalism are hot topics of discussion. These words can be used synonymously with each other. Multiculturalism was spawned from affirmative action. Its roots are deeply intertwined to the Civil Rights Movement. Multiculturalism is a concept that deals with understanding and responding to challenges associated with racial diversity, such as college admissions and employment (Nieto, 1992).

Although the modern version of the affirmative action idea was derived from John F. Kennedy's executive order in 1961, it was not signed into law until 1964 by his successor Lyndon Johnson. The Civil Rights Act outlawed race, color, religious, sex, or nationality discrimination (Fuchs, 2015).

Some people in the American society insist that racism no longer exists, and there is no need for programs such as affirmative action. Although this idea is spun around media circles, this is simply not the case. Today racial minorities still face racism in institutions of higher learning and in the job market (Bertrand and Mullainathan, 2004). To a multicultural student the difference in the achievement gap and college preparedness could make one feel very marginalized in their position on and off campus, in relation to the status quo, because they lack basic needs to be successful.

Another action that can cause multicultural students to feel very marginalized on a university's campus is realizing the playing field was never level or equal. For instance, in 2004, Elizabeth Paige Laurie, the heir to the Walmart fortune, paid her roommate, Elena Martinez, 20,000 dollars to do all her university coursework, and she was awarded a degree (Glaister, 2004). Now, in 2019, academia has been rocked with a college admission scandal. Fifty parents, coaches, and test proctors were charged in this debacle. Rick Singer, who prosecutors deemed the mastermind, promoted cheating on college entrance exams and bribing coaches to give well to do students an outright advantage to getting into their perspective college of choice (Morales & I, 2019). Also, only one school held the parents and the students accountable for this injustice, Stanford University. In addition, a recent study has discovered that Harvard's Legacy and Athlete Preferences from 2009-2014, found that the athletes, legacy alumni children, and children of donors and faculty who gained admittance were all Caucasian. 43% of the students at Harvard get preferential admissions. Only 1/3 could have achieved admissions on their own accord (Weissman, 2019). These students did not have the grades but they had access and came from extremely wealthy families who may be alumni of those particular colleges or universities. The above examples were an illustrated microcosm of a much bigger problem. One has to ask, how big is this issue and how long has this issue infiltrated academia?

Another area where the idea of student multiculturalism is failing is at the curricular level. According to the National Center of Education Statistics, there are 10.5 million Caucasian students enrolled at higher education campuses along with 9.4 million minorities. The demographic of the universities and colleges in the U.S. are very diverse and with that diversity a change to the curriculum should be in order. The significance of producing a diverse curriculum would positively change the attitudes and perceptions of all cultures that it represents (Leslie & Leslie, 1972). Students who took part in courses designed around the idea of multiculturalism indicated a level of multicultural competence, equity in their educational pursuit, and more interaction with students from other cultures (Aberson, 2007). Also, 500 first-year university students, who had access to information and activities pertaining to other racial groups as part of a class Indicated on a survey that there is a huge amount of racial inequity in the U.S. (Lopez, 2004).

Furthermore, the white male supremacy issue on college campuses is a huge factor that adds to the failure of the idea of student multiculturalism. It is counter-intuitive to the Caucasian way of life and study. Although most campuses will say they are diverse on paper but if you take a closer look, you will find displays of the supremacist dominance everywhere, such as, in the media images, in the façade and the use of racial capital campaigns, in faulty admission policies aimed at keeping the percentage of diverse students low versus their white counterparts, as well as, in campuses leading attacks on affirmative action. Everyday diverse students are being attacked by discriminatory acts and this action again leads to a negative impact on learning with peers and in a campus environment. Also, at Harvard University between December

2018 through March 2019, anonymous derogatory text messages were sent to 80 minority students. The emails included racial taunts such as, horse face, you don't belong here, you are just here because of affirmative action so get the fuck out, and etc. These students went to the dean and the police with their complaints. The dean could not divulge any information about the investigation due to Family Educational Rights and Privacy Act. After a few months the university released a statement informing the students neither the police nor Harvard's investigations could determine who sent the demeaning text messages. No other students received these types of messages on campus (Vu, 2019). In another example, in November of 2015, at Harvard's Law school, students walked into Wasserstein Hall to find portraits of their black tenured professors with black tape covering them up. At the time, some students called it a hate crime. The dean of the school revealed the school has a race problem. Although the dean acknowledged there is a race problem at Harvard's law school, Alan Dershowitz, a law professor, denies they have one. In an interview with the magazine, the Business Insider, he states, "The last thing these students want is diversity," "They may want superficial diversity, because for them diversity is a code word for 'more of us" (Graham, 2015).

Conclusion

In conclusion, today there are so many different attacks on affirmative action, Title VI, and Title IX you would think these were a type of modern-day Jim Crow. These laws were brought into existence to level the playing field so to speak, to give everyone a fair share at life, liberty, and the pursuit of happiness.

Abraham Lincoln signed the Emancipation Proclamation in 1863. It declared that all persons held as slaves shall be free. This became a symbol of hope for all African Americans at the time. Many years later, Martin Luther King Jr. gave his famous I have a dream speech in Washington. He conveyed to the people, that after many years, since the signing of the Emancipation Proclamation, the Negro is still not free. He conveyed they are still snared by segregation, discrimination, and poverty. He continued to inform the crowd that the Negro and other proponents that are entrapped by injustice will never be satisfied until racism, police brutality, and basic dignity are restored.

Since the 1987 statements of Al Campanis, on the issue of race in sport, we have come a long way in the consideration of paying college athletes to play. Some may find comfort knowing that it is on the docket for discussion in today's world. While others may find it discomforting because we have not gone far enough even though it's been proven that the NCAA has been in violation of the 1890 Sherman Act, better known as anti-trust infringement.

THE FALLACY

"I know you won't believe me, but the highest form of human excellence is to question oneself and others."

~ Socrates

BIG NAMESFOR IT and BIG NAMES AGAINST paying athletes

Since the signing of SB 206 and the NCAA's stunning reversal in favor of paying athletes to play there has been some back in forth between athletes and people on the issue. Some for pay to play and some against pay to play.

For instance, Jeremy Bloom, a former Colorado University CU football player and Olympic skier, stated that he is in favor of California's SB 206. He believes the NCAA's decision to pay athletes based upon their NIL was done to take the focus away from pending congressional and state legislation. He further comments that for more than 50 years the NCAA has been rolling out the snake oil, and now people are not willing to listen to them anymore. He also conveys that he has been surprised by the NCAA's decision to allow certain athletes the ability to collect money from playing while denying others. Case in point, Drew Henson, an amateur football player at the University of Michigan, who also played professional baseball was granted the ability to collect a couple million dollars from his professional sport and keep it while playing college football. In addition, he does not believe college sport is exactly amateur anymore. For instance, Florida state fired Willie Taggart as football head coach and gave him 17 million to leave. Other coaches are getting hired and fired for millions of dollars, and television contracts are worth billions. He further states that everyone is getting paid except the athletes who provide the entertainment. It is pretty ironic (Metivier & Barsch, 2019).

THE FALLACY

Similar to Jeremy Bloom is the plight of Katelyn Ohasi. In October 2019, she released a short video chronicling her feelings toward the NCAA and her approval of the Fair Pay to Play Act. She stated that in the last meet of her senior year she scored a prefect ten in floor gymnastics. Her routine went viral with 100 million people tuning in to watch the performance, yet she explains that she was unable to capitalize on budding opportunities that arose from the exposure. She further explained the NCAA rules shackled her and prevented her from entering in to any lucrative monetary agreements. She continued to explain what a difference it would had made if she was able to capitalize off here NIL since she had no professional league to join. In addition, she stated that the Fair Pay to Play Act is not about salaries, it's about enabling the student athletes to control their own destiny in regard to their NIL. It's also about ensuring student athletes are paid accordingly if their jersey is still being sold in the bookstore 10 years after they have graduated. Another item in regard to pay to play you have to consider is the fact that only 4% of all media coverage focuses on women. Also, it is about respecting and seeing student athletes and college students as equals where they are afforded the same rights to be compensated for their original work and skill (Crouse & Stockton, 2019).

Another person for pay to play is Senator Mitt Romney. "We're coming for you," meaning Congress will act on the issue of pay to play, which put the NCAA on notice that their policies in regard to pay to play need to change. He continued to say that it isn't fair that college athletes are not receiving any pay, due to the amount of time and effort they give to the sport. Although Mitt Romney supports pay to play, he does not want a few athletes driving Italian supercars while other athletes are having a hard time supporting themselves. NIL needs to be regulated to a certain extent. He also goes on to state that the college sports market needs to be diversified so every school can benefit (Romboy, 2019).

Even one of the NCAA's own, Walter Byers, the longest serving executive director, was for paying athletes. He stated 35 years ago, "The structure we have in place as a means of controlling the activities of recruiting and financial aid must go through a dramatic change. Is there anything that can keep big-time college athletics operating within the rules? That's the real question. I'm gradually coming to the conclusion that there has to be a major rearrangement on the part of the institutions of higher learning as to what they want to do with their athletic programs .... It's the Me Generation. It's mine and I want it now. Well, why not? I think back in time. It used to be that a rich alumnus could get a needy kid out of a Gary, Indiana steel mill and send him to Yale. Then the NCAA came along with a bunch of rules and said, 'You can't do that.' An alumnus can't send a kid to school to play athletics? But is it wrong for the donor to give the boy the money? No, I'm feeling that it's only the colleges with the rules that say it's wrong. The coaches don't think it's so wrong anymore. The public doesn't think it's so wrong (McCallum, 1984)."

On the other hand, Cody McDavis, a former college basketball player from the University of Northern Colorado and now an attorney at UCLA school of law, is against paying athletes to play. He believes playing college sports is a dream for most, and if we start paying athletes now that puts that dream at risk. He further states that there have been millions of kids who dedicated their lives to sport. College has always been the entry point for that dream. Trying to win a full ride scholarship is the goal. Once that is achieved, students take part in college athletics for four years, receive their degree, and begin their professional lives. College sports is about the love of the game not the money. Any compensation would result in less opportunities for non-football and non-basketball athletes (McDavis, 2019).

Likewise, Gene Smith, Ohio state athletic director and one of two administrative personnel working with the NCAA in determining athletes NIL rights, has come out against SB 206. He states that his worry stems from the broad parameters that were set for paying college athletes. He further conveys that it is somehow difficult for athletic directors to figure out how to regulate intercollegiate sport. He states, "One of our principles is try to create rules and regulations to try and achieve fair play (Aschoff, 2019)."

THE FALLACY

In another example, while answering Stephen A. Smith, an ESPN reporter in an interview, Tim Tebow commented on California's SB 206 Fair Pay to Play Act and its implications. He stated when he was in college his football jersey was one of the top selling jerseys' behind Kobe Bryant's and LeBron James' around the world. He insists he did not make a cent from the sales, and he did not want to anyway. This is due to the fact; he believes college is about supporting your team and your university. College was also about where my family wanted to go and about my grandfather's dream that the University of Florida would win the FCC championship. Paying student athletes would take that passion away. Paying athletes will change the college environment to an everything is about me culture from a college environment of us or we. He continued by voicing that we live in a culture of selfishness and paying student athletes would add to it (#FirstTake, 2019).

In conclusion, from the information provided two key pertinent questions should be asked. One being, how will SB 206 and the NCAA's decision to let outside entities compensate intercollegiate student athletes affect the strategic planning in post-secondary institutions?

Two being, how will letting outside entities compensate intercollegiate student athletes affect human and racial capital campaigns on post-secondary institutions? Once the statute and the NCAA's ordinance are enacted, a rich plethora of data will begin to materialize and change the nature of post-secondary institutions. This action will be deliberated and debated on for years and years to come.

THE FALLACY

*"Failure isn't fatal, but failure
to change might be."*

~ John Wooden

THE PLAN

The recommendations suggested here come by the way of two scenarios that may become relevant and a reality for most, if not all, post-secondary institutions and students that participate in intercollegiate sports.

Scenario one

Scenario one addresses question one; How will SB 206 and the NCAA's decision to let outside entities compensate intercollegiate student athletes affect the strategic planning in post-secondary institutions?

In strategic planning, much like the game of chess, one must evaluate his or her position, formulate a plan, and develop his or her minor pieces, and protect the king. The goal of chess is to establish an imbalance. An imbalance in the game of chess is any difference in two opposing positions. An imbalance is not a winning position, it is just a variation in a position. It is the responsibility of players to create an advantageous position (Silman, 1993).

Before delving into how the strategic planning in post-secondary institutions will be affected by SB 206 and the NCAA 's decision to let outside entities compensate intercollegiate student athletes, we will define the term strategic planning. Webster's Encyclopedic Unabridged Dictionary of the English Language defines strategic as forming an integral part of a stratagem. A stratagem is defined as a plan to achieve a goal (Webster's, 1989). In 1965, Ansoff in his seminal work contemplated the term strategic in relation to an organization and its environment. So, questions associated with the internal or external environment should be looked upon in a strategic manner. Buckland defined strategy as the action in which businesses engage in coordinated managed activities in order to reach their institution's goals (Buckland, 2009).

On the other hand, planning is a crucial component of a business' alliance to the organization as whole, to people who work there, to individuals who use their services, and to the community at large (Beere et al., 2011). Another researcher by the name of Rizatti states that planning is a procedure that benefits human behavior by aiding effective and sensible decision making in regard to organizational objectives.

In 1993, Goodstein et al., illuminated the idea that strategic planning is a method in which business entities forecast the future and create practices and enterprising activities needed to reach their goals. Higher Education Institutions HEI use strategic planning to estimate the cost and expense of future anticipated changes. According to Meyer et al, strategic planning is needed to stay competitive in regard to resources, reputation, attractiveness to students, and community engagement. As mentioned earlier, goals and objectives are extremely important to the strategic planning process. Today strategic planners use smart goals and objectives. Smart goals and objectives are Specific, Measurable, Assignable, Realistic, and Time-related. For example, the goals and objectives must be precise and quantifiable. In addition, they are practical and sometimes inter-changeable. Also, they are initiated with a time constraint (Doran, 1981). Beyond the goals and objectives, strategic planning must be collaborative. Collaborative Strategic Planning (CSP), although very similar to other planning approaches, can prove to be more effective by the use of eight characteristics generated through the social interaction of a selected Planning Task Force (PTF). The PTF is a group selected for their hardiness to the task of CSP. This group will inspire change by the organization of ideas it generates through interaction with their peers and other stakeholders. The eight characteristics that the PTF will produce are meaningful engagement, transparency, divergence of ideas, proprietorship of the planning process and outcomes, reflective thinking and refinements, exploration and learning, an independent perspective, and connectivity with the community they serve.

Meaningful engagement

In the past, the information derived from surveys and questionnaires have been used to engage members of the strategic planning committee. They were seen as valid tools. For example, they can be used in determining your committee and possibly determining critical information conveyed by the community and or stakeholders. Although this is true, in CSP, the committee engages in face to face interaction and critical discussions, thus meaningful engagement.

Transparency

In regard to the information collected during the CSP process, the committee, community, and stakeholders have total access to the information generated through this collaborative process. This includes the decision-making process and access to financial statements and records.

Divergence of Ideas

In CSP, all members of the committee share in the responsibility to bring forth thought provoking relevant discussions, information, and interesting perspectives that lead to positive outcomes.

Proprietorship of the planning process and outcomes

The committee or the PTF, are vested members in the process of devising a strategic planning. Their resources of time, skill, and knowledge are vital to the production of a viable plan that will lead the university for the next five years.

Reflective thinking and refinements

The PTF are always receiving new information, due to the on-going data collection going on during the CSP process. When this happens, the committee has to make adjustments. One
way to make adjustments is to be reflective and then refine strategies that apply to certain outcomes.

Exploration and learning

In regard to exploration and learning, the PTF, learn how to participate in share aspirations, missions, visions, and goals.

Independent perspective

The PTF committee focuses on creating outcomes alongside their peers. They consult best practices when determining the direction of their planning. They could use surveys and questionnaires and other tools to help with this process.

Connectivity with the community

PTF members are committed to transparency. During the CSP process open dialogue with the community is very much necessary. Another name for this process is informed dreaming. When this happens, a bridge is formed between the university and the community which transforms to trust (Sanaghan, (2009).

Now since strategic planning is fully defined, we will bring to light the issue of how letting outside entities compensate intercollegiate student athletes will affect the strategic planning in post-secondary institutions. The excerpt of William Ernest Hensley's Invictus poem brilliantly illuminates the transformation of having no rights to a position of being able to control how their NIL is used with the lines, "Out of the night that covers me, Black as a pit from pole to pole, I thank whatever gods may be for my unconquerable soul .... I am the Master of my Fate, I am the Captain of my Soul."

It would be farfetched to believe that student athletes would be the only ones benefiting from the changes in the law. Savvy college goers also would be watching and want to take part in this marketing opportunity. With anyone able to benefit from NIL, everyone will be acting as a free agent on post-secondary campuses. This is similar to what Curt Flood did in baseball, to secure the rights for future players to negotiate trade, contract, and salary agreements. Now students and student athletes will be able to venture into various contracts, as well as, trademark NIL's and solicit salary agreements. This will undoubtedly hit the budgets and the marketability of higher education institutions. These institutions will now have to contend with the idea that athletes and students are people not property or robots to be manipulated no matter what is in the student handbook. They will be invited to strategic planning sessions and seen as equals commanding a social media understanding and stardom, lucrative apparel contracts, as well as financial wealth. Although they will not be seen as worthy by the boards, chancellors, presidents, chairs, and the like, these young entrepreneurs will wield power stemming from their social media followers which can and will affect enrollment, diversity, sports, and community perceptions of the college and university campuses.

For instance, in 2012, Facebook had 1 billion users and on average 584 million people converge on Facebook daily. In the same year, Twitter had over 140 million active users with 300,000 new users enrolling daily. On average there were 750 tweets shared per second and 175 million tweets transpiring on busy days (Raphael, 2012). Currently, in 2019, Facebook has 2.41 billion subscribers that are active, and Instagram has one billion subscribers. Twitter commands 330 million subscribers and growing (Clement, 2019). Twitter, Instagram, and etc. have boosted the development of new digital

platforms that have given way to a variety of employment opportunity, as well as, different approaches to communicate and disperse information. Twitter and Instagram are the most prominent micro blogging platforms that allow for fast short message outputs and circulations (Walker et al., 2017). Twitter and Instagram facilitate real time conversation. One researcher illustrates the main difference between the two micro-blogging platforms Twitter and Instagram from Facebook; Facebook is a scene from your living room where you are watching TV and switching channels represents you catching up with your friends and family by commenting on what is posted on their page (channel). As for Twitter and Instagram, they represent the bar scene where lots and lots people are interacting, some you want and some you don't want. They are interacting in
real time and commenting on anything that interests them in a particular moment (Mueller).

Up until recently, only athletic departments were heavily concerned with social media. Social media has been a tool used for marketing and branding. They can be construed as one in the same (Blazka et al., 2018).

The main outcome of branding is to achieve a meaningful divergence between an entity and consumer. This difference, if communicated correctly, will be perceived and received positively with value. Ultimately, it will translate into loyalty and a feeling of community and unity with a particular group the brand is associated with (Keller, 2003). Coaches use it for recruiting, and sport information departments have consistently used it for publicizing statistics, game information, ticket information, media affiliations, and team biographies and match ups (Stoldt & Vermillion, 2013). Clemson University, a leader in the use and promotion of social media, spends $160 thousand dollars to support their efforts of digital engagement. Their strategy is to engage fans and recruits by having a lot of supporting web content (Thamell, 2017). If post-secondary institutions are to survive, all departments need to become well versed in the use of social media platforms and develop policies for the use of students and athletes that do not infringe on their new found rights of having control of their NIL.

Another issue that will affect the strategic planning of higher education institutions based upon letting outside entities compensate intercollegiate student athletes is trademark infringement. Savvy athletes and students alike, now possibly commanding significant amounts of money, can venture into trademarking words, phrase, poses, dances, in regard to their NIL. For example, in 2013, JMAN2 Enterprises Limited Liability Company LLC., the licensing company of Jonny Manziel A.K.A. Johnny Football, filled a lawsuit against Eric Vaughn. Eric Vaughn had been merchandising shirts utilizing Texas A&M's color scheme with the phrase "Keep Calm and Johnny Football." In the previous year, right after winning the Heisman Trophy, John Manziel had applied and received a trademark for the name Johnny Football. His company petitioned the court for trademark infringement and won. The NCAA stated that Manziel could keep any of the proceeds he was awarded by the court. Jeremy Lin and Tim Tebow have been other athletes who have done the same thing (Grady & Nagel, 2013). Post-secondary institutions will have to execute a great deal of restraint and due diligence when thinking about using a phrase, word, or the like to avoid costly law suits brought by students or student athletes. This will affect strategic planning due to the fact that it will alter how they plan, engage, and budget for initiatives.

As a result of not being on the threshold of SB 206, some athletes, such as, Simone Manual, the Olympic goal medalist, decided to forgo her last year as a student athlete at Stanford and follow Katie Ledecky in turning professional and branding herself through a lucrative sponsorship. The Simone Manual line of goggles and suits, were designed "to empower and inspire all people to dream big, dream bold, and dream beyond, through designs that reflect the joy of swimming", according to TYR (Slear, 2020).

*"Don't be trapped by dogma
which is living with the results of other people's thinking."*

~ Steve Jobs

SCENARIO TWO

Scenario two addresses question two; How will letting outside entities compensate intercollegiate student athletes affect human and racial capital campaigns on post-secondary institutions?

We will begin our discussion by dissecting the question and answering it piece by piece starting with the issue of racial capital campaigns.

The race card, a phrase popularized during the 1990's, has been deemed one of the most overused terms related to race. Playing the race card is a type of rhetorical behavior that is deceitful and disgraceful. It is defined as a coercive action in which a person or persons proposition a scheme to entice racial pride or prejudice in order to cause a person or a group of people to act contrary to what is ordinarily expected. Also, the race card has been construed as a form of tokenism devised to coax a community into believing an institution is advancing a cause or a position of power for people of color, yet this proves to be contrary to their true intention which is to diffuse any negative publicity or negative feelings towards that particular institution (The Journal of Blacks in Higher Education, 1998).

Twenty-one years later, the race card is still being played but under a different guise, racial capital or capitalism. As mentioned in chapter one, racial capital/ism is defined as the process of deriving social or economic value from the racial identity of another (Leong, 2013). An example of this would be an administrator at an institution not known for its diversity or troubled by the lack of the diversity on his or her campus okays the use of photoshop to replace a Caucasian student with a minority student to show that they are a diverse campus. In another example, the sale of basketball and football jerseys from mostly African American athletes are sold for over $100 in college and university bookstores, but who are the benefactors of their sales, if it is not the athletes?

When student athletes begin to venture into a lucrative clothing and merchandising campaign with outside entities, post-secondary higher education institutions will cease to have the same marketing clout they once had over the sales and profits of products, due to the fact, companies, such as, Nike, Adidas, and the like will develop products for those particular student athletes they have a contract with and then share the profits. Racial capital campaigns on post-secondary institutions will be affected by ceasing to exist due to the athletes NIL rights. Most racial capital campaigns centered around athletes only deal with one or two athletes. The institution places giant photo banners of the athlete all over campus, and it gives the on-looker the sense of being a part of a winning team, due to the fact they are looking at a winning athlete that happens to be a part of a minority group. Letting outside entities compensate intercollegiate student athletes in regard to their NIL will begin to cost the post-secondary institutions for the use of those NIL rights. Those same NIL rights are already extended to all college students. If the college students are savvy, they will begin to ask for compensation every time the college or university wants to use their NIL rights for photos, websites, and or social media posts. This will surely thrust higher education institutions into the use of websites, such as, Shutterstock, Adobe stock, and etc., to use photos and or videos. Again, savvy students who understand supply and demand will begin to post photos and videos for sale on these same sights. Post-secondary institutions will have no choice but to invest in these products so they can continue to publicly market their institution.

Now, we will discuss the second part of question two, how human capital will be affected on post-secondary campuses by letting outside entities compensate intercollegiate student athletes. Human capital is defined as an investment oforganizations in education and training to increase employees' knowledge, expertise, and skills, which ultimately may maximize organizational productivity and outputs (Becker, 1993). With the rise of student athletes NIL rights and wealth, higher education institutions may begin to invest in wealth management courses that can instruct young minority athletes how to invest and protect their financial assets.

Thinking along those same lines, post-secondary administrators may begin to pursue a minority workforce to assist these student athletes in the management of their wealth and their education. This could lead to a movement to hire and tenure more minority faculty members. Minority faculty members are supposed to be seen as role models and or mentors to minority students. Mentors are supposed to encourage the students that they divulge knowledge to, as well as, provide information pertaining to academic study, research, scholarship, and internship opportunities. Minority faculty members sometimes are looked upon as the beacon of hope and security on a campus of insecurity for minority students. Their presence can help guide students away from academic pitfalls. Also, their support can influence attitudes and behaviors of minority students, thus building students' confidences and strengths. For minorities that enter graduate programs, they frequently report that the Caucasian professor and classmates display passive aggressive attitudes towards them which can be construed as disrespect and discrimination (Harris, Janovec, Murray, Gubbala, & Robinson, 2018).

On American campuses, it is rare to a see a minority faculty member that is tenured and full-time (Moody, 2004). For example, at Penn State, faculty has been 3% African - American for 30 years (Henderson, 2018). Furthermore, minorities are not mentored and therefore, they face many obstacles when trying to get published. Most of the time they are excluded within the departmental network. Moody speculates that this type of disenfranchisement causes minorities to doubt how they are proceeding in goal attainment in relation to tenure. According to Womack and Morgan (1995) "The prerequisites for tenure and salary increments should be uniformed and posted so faculty members aren't misled by the specifications". Most universities do not want the qualifications uniformed or posted, due to the fact, they retain the option to promote or deny tenure salary increases based upon their own subjective judgements when people come up for review. It is surprising to think that student athletes' NIL rights, in relation to their compensation by outside entities, could have a huge impact on the hiring and tenure of minorities, but this might be the catalyst and the push higher education needs in its pursuit to become more equitable.

THE FALLACY

EPILOGUE

In the section entitled "The Plan," I suggested the need for strategic planning when SB 206 is enacted. The real questions are- What does that look like? What does this accomplish? How are students going to be affected, and how does post-secondary institutions move from a place of comfort to the future while staying in the black (no pun intended) related to the budget.

Most if not all of these questions can be answered through the Collaborative Strategic Planning CSP process. Collaborative Strategic Planning CSP is about change. Positive change that can and will lead your organization into the future. Change is very similar to a coin. A coin has two sides but each side looks very different from one another. When change is introduced to people their response is like the coin. Some can deal with it while some cannot.

To illustrate this point, we will refer to the classic "Who Moved My Cheese?" by Spencer Johnson. The story follows four mice called Sniff, Scurry, Hem, and Haw. Everyday these mice maneuver through a maze to get to Station C in order to receive food. Over time there was less and less cheese found at Station C until there was none. Sniff and Scurry were hip to these changes and when the day came when there was no more cheese to be found at Station C, Sniff and Scurry took off running in search of food. The other two mice, Hem and Haw, were not paying attention to the small changes in their cheese ration. So, when the day came that there was no cheese Hem screamed, and Haw was telling himself that this was not happening. Therefore, you may want to leave the Hem's and the Haw's of your institution off your team as they will have problems adapting to change. Also, to learn about your team members, you may want to survey them to discover their strengths, weaknesses, and personality types.

Collaborative Strategic Planning CSP is also a catalyst to leadership. The President entrusts a small group of people working together to institute a mission, a vision, and to execute goals and objectives. This allows them to move forward in creating diverse campus cultures and climates. When SB 206 is enacted the mission, vision, goals and objectives of post-secondary institutions will most certainly change.

For example, in chapter two of another classic book, "Make Your Bed," Admiral McRaven talks about changing the world, but insists you cannot do this alone. You need a team you can rely on who have bought into the mission and vision of your goals and objectives. Admiral McRaven implicitly drives this point home with this short example. When he was competing to become a seal, if he or members of his team would become sick, due to the cold, the flu, or exhaustion he or his team members picked up the slack. They paddled harder on the boats, gave up portions of their food ration, and if there was any digging needed, they dug harder and deeper to cover the ailing team member's portion of work to complete the daily mission. They all had different strengths but what makes them special is the bond and the level of commitment they had to the team and the mission. Keep this point in mind.

Once your team is assembled, it may a good idea to form a focus group and then complete a student athlete community needs assessment. This is done to understand the priorities and interests of the athletes pertaining to the post-secondary institution. Due diligence is needed here. This is about athletics so you must include the athletic directors, athletic compliance officers, and student athletes. Prudence must be used to ensure members of your cash cow sports (basketball, football, and etc.) are on your team, first and foremost. Also, ensure that the demographic matches the participation. So, if your men's and women's basketball teams are 85% African American, it probably is a good idea to place an African American on the strategic planning team. Although this is true, take it with a grain a salt. There are always exceptions to the rule, but make sure it is warranted. Then pull from the other sports to elicit a different perspective since this will ultimately affect all athletes on campus.

After the need's assessment is completed, guidelines should be introduced to direct and curtail months and even years of planning on this particular topic. The results of the needs assessment must be incorporated into these guidelines. The dictionary concludes that guidelines are suggestions for a future course of action, hence a direction.

There are three items that I am including to direct your thought process on this particular subject matter to ensure relevancy to your planning session. They are succession from the NCAA, athletic unionizing, and incorporation of the athletic departments. The caveat is that this is a starting point and not an end all be all list. Again, you may have these items on your list, then again, your list may be different. Due to the size and the level of commitment to sport, the items may be pertinent for some but less pertinent for others. Post-secondary institutions along with other educational organizations should not subscribe to the one size fits all notion unless they themselves enjoy playing Russian roulette with annual budgets which could lead to the financial ruin of an organization.

We will address them one at a time in no particular order of importance. Also, in the interest of time, these items will be discussed in brevity.

NCAA Succession

As mentioned in the first chapter of this book, in 1906, thirty-six post-secondary schools enacted the Intercollegiate Athletic Association IAA which later became the National Collegiate Athletic Association NCAA in 1910. It would seem that the institutions didn't care what happened in relation to rules or whom controlled policy at that time. The inaction by these institutions can be construed as complacency, due to the fact, their only concern was the revenues that sport, mainly football was bringing in. So, if an outside organization swooped in with given power and authority, they did not care because it did not affect their balance sheets.

So, today is the day to take responsibility for your inaction over a century ago. You can't blame the millennials. This was caused by a small group of universities who were unwilling at the time to give up their advantage and monopoly that they had on intercollegiate sports and other non-Ivy league university systems. At this point in time, the NCAA needs post-secondary institutions, athletic departments, and their fans more than they need it. Before the onset of Covid-19, the NCAA would take in $14 billion dollars a year. What if they didn't exist? You need to figure that $14 billion dollars split between institutions of higher education would keep everyone in the black for a long period of time unless there is mismanagement of funds. If you really think about it, the university and colleges systems could create a new national sport organization model. The athletic directors are in place along with compliance officers and most importantly the athletes. The post-secondary institutions are just missing a plan, guidelines, and action. Don't miss the boat like Hem and Haw.

Unionizing Athletes

Why should athletes unionize? It's simple! When paid or unpaid labor band together they can improve conditions for all labor performers. They could demand better benefits, such as, long term medical treatment, the re-enactment of the four-year grant in aid scholarship, ensure equitable living conditions are mandated and attained, and seek accountability, internally and externally. In addition, they could pursue liability protections while lobbying for laws, bylaws, and policy changes. Finally, they could be provided legal advice, representation, wealth management training, and advisement when needed (aflcio, 2020).

THE FALLACY

Lest we forget, how the term student athlete came into existence, or how Dr. Richard Strauss, or Jerry Sandusky, or even Larry Nassar abused athletes. Where was the accountability? In each instance the universities escaped real punishment by accepting a slap on the rest such as probation, if they got any punishment at all. Or we can look at the current situation of college sports as post-secondary institutions are rushing to re-open while Covid-19 is spiking throughout the United States. More than 130,000 people have lost their lives to the disease to date, yet the show must go on. Athletes are going to be placing their lives on the line this fall for what? Not for the love of the game, but for some organization's profit margin which is somewhere in the neighborhood of $4 billion dollars. When is enough, enough? If the organization which is supposed to protect these athletes will not do the right thing, maybe the intercollegiate athletes will collectively. Yes! Although members of congress has suggested an athletic bill of rights, this should be solely about athletes no politics (Berkowitz, 2020).

Incorporation

Athletic departments incorporating may be a way for institutions and athletic departments to co-exist separate from one another. If an athletic department incorporates as a non-profit it could solicit grant funds and donations similarly to the institutions. Also, speaking about the budgets, if any funds are left over at the end of the academic year, instead of re-distributing funds back into the institution's main budget, the athletic department could invest those remaining funds in the interest of becoming self-sufficient. They could begin to sell and promote products that are tax deductible such as, ticket sales, apparel, and other merchandises. They could venture into lucrative TV, radio, social media, and streaming service contracts, as mentioned in "The Plan." This will allow the athletic departments to create their own TV, social media, and media channels. With all these new products there will be a greater need for marketing, licensing, trademarking, as well as, copyrighting to hinder unlawful usage and piracy. Do these actions and tactics sound familiar? What's good for the goose is good for the gander.

Conclusion

In conclusion, when we think of strategies that could possibly lead an institution of higher education into the future, we need to be strategic in planning and in our thinking. The top down approach of doing business is almost non-existence in successful companies these days. Now organizations welcome outside of the box thinking from all levels of the organization to stay relevant, as well as, looking around the industry and developing best practices to align their marketing and products with others in the same business. With that in mind, Maya Angelou has a quote which reads, "If you don't like something, change it. If you can't change it, change your attitude." Translation, this epilogue is about change. Some people in your organization will be apprehensive to change. Thus, a percentage of those people will either try to sabotage your efforts and the venture or opt to leave your organization all together. The ones who decide to stay will have to adjust their mindset in relation to the organization's new mission and vision.

END

THE FALLACY

A Noteworthy review by a former athlete

What do you like about the book?
"It's No Fun When the Rabbit's Got the Gun"... The Fallacy does a great job of illustrating the "Gift and the Curse" of Capitalism within the NCAA, and those that have enjoyed the "gravy train" to themselves for so long, will now have to share with the very athletes they've exploited. But there's a new day coming with SB 206, and Amateur or Collegiate Athletes are now taking matters into their own hands.

Was there anything that stands out to you about the information presented in the book?
The book does a great job of pointing out the origin "Greek term Athlete, History of the NCAA and Amateurism bringing light to the rampant commercialized environment that continues to thrive for everyone except the college athlete! As a former 4 year "full ride" collegiate athlete myself (which doesn't even exist anymore) and graduate of DePaul University a High Div 1 Basketball Program that was had a Top10-20 rank every year and actually was No. #3 in the country my Freshman Year going into the NCAA Tournament. I can recall times that my teammates and I would piece money together to buy a pizza on late nights after going to class all day, practice/weight training, then afterwards study hall, and if you didn't get food before 10pm, there wasn't anything on campus that was open. During this time Domino's Pizza had come on the scene with the business model of "Delivery in 30 minutes or less or your Pizza is Free"... as you can imagine, we longed for those days when the driver was late, free Pizza had extra flavor for a starving athlete!!

On a scale of 1-4, with four being highly recommended....
4. I would highly recommend "Fallacy" a must read, especially for Parents / Kids with athletic scholarship potential!!

THE FALLACY

I don't think most people have an idea of what a day / life of collegiate athletes look like, not to mention the expectations and pressures to consistently perform at a high level. Yet go to school / classes, keep up with course work loads, homework, presentations, labs etc. required and continue to practice and get better. With that said, whether these teams have great success or not, each year these institutions, coaches, and others (everyone except the "collegiate athlete", or "product" themselves are compensated with long/short term business relationships that are very lucrative! The athlete is told to be grateful for a "free education" and some school gear/clothes from sponsors. While no one mentions the "tremendous bodily risk" each athlete exposes themselves to daily to be the best they can be and constantly put their body in harms' way and/or rigorous training that does have residual damage over time!

Their fellow students on campus on academic scholarship or not, go to class, and get to enjoy every aspect of the college experience without those same pressure and/or risk, only the pressures of themselves to graduate and maybe their parents or family giving financial support. While choosing to work, and have a job gaining experience in the workplace and your signed jersey, t-shirt, or tickets given!

However, every collegiate athlete given a scholarship has an intrinsic value to that program. It is ironic and simply put, the fact that someone other than the athlete has been profiting and now making policy/decisions on their NIL rights is exploitation! The long time coming and paramount SB 206 has many views. opinions, etc. about what's fair, right/wrong, etc. but at the end of the day the powers that be see the 14+ multi-billion dollar industry they've been able to exploit for so long in jeopardy as the "Sniff / Scurry" take control of their NIL future/destiny seeking alternative options (i.e., Bball players going overseas out of High School, 1 and Done's) and the "Hem's/Haw's may complain but will be grateful for whatever they do/don't get skipping/transferring schools every year or two...

I remember having this conversation with a parent of a High School quarterback and telling him how the "college education" was overrated and any athlete, especially a future High 1st Round draft pick, is risking their financial livelihood to continue going to college when a piece of paper guarantees them nothing (0), no work experience, no job, nothing but questions of what now? When in fact if you know you will be a middle to high draft pick, you're guaranteed a certain amount of money for likely a 3+ year contract, and that even after 10 years in a regular working career choice you still couldn't match that amount of income! Not to mention future contracts, exposure to other opportunities, endorsements, and business relationships and total control of your NIL!!

There are so many different issues that can and will be an open conversation from your book, much needed to bring light to the collegiate athlete's plight, Thank You!!!

- Kevin Holland, DePaul University (1987-1991)

GLOSSARY

ACT: American College Testing ACT exam is used as an entrance exam by most of the college and universities around the nation. They use your scores from the ACT to make an admissions decision. The ACT test measures the high school student's readiness for college by testing their knowledge on subjects such as English, Math, Reading, Science, and Writing.

Affirmative Action: employment policy and law for increased representation for minority groups.

American Civil Liberties Union: the American Civil Liberties Union was founded in 1920 and is our nation's guardian of liberty. The ACLU works in the courts, legislatures and communities to defend and preserve the individual rights and liberties guaranteed to all people in this country by the Constitution and laws of the United States.

Assimilation: the merging of cultural traits from previously distinct cultural group.

Black Lives Matter: The Black Lives Matter Global Network is a chapter-based, member led organization whose mission is to build local power and to intervene in violence inflicted on Black communities by the state and vigilantes.

Blue Lives Matter: In today's evolving society, an increasing number of citizens fail to accept responsibility for their actions and attempt to escape the consequences through outward blame. Due to the nature of the profession, law enforcement personnel are seen as easy targets andare consequently bullied

by slander, illegitimate complaints, frivolous law suits, and physical threats. The goal of Blue Lives Matter is to honor and recognize the actions of law enforcement to strengthen the public support of an
understandably naive society.

Brown versus the Board of Education: Brown v. Board of Education of Topeka was a landmark 1954 Supreme Court case in which the justices ruled
unanimously that racial segregation of children in public schools was unconstitutional.
Brown v. Board of Education was one of the cornerstones of the civil rights movement,
and helped establish the precedent that "separate-but-equal" education and other services were not, in fact, equal at all.

Chess: A game of strategy played by two persons, each with sixteen pieces on a chessboard.

Civil Rights Act: The Civil Rights Act of 1964, which ended segregation in public places and banned employment discrimination on the basis of race, color, religion, sex or national origin, is considered one of the crowning legislative achievements of the
civil rights movement. First proposed by President John F. Kennedy, it survived strong opposition from southern members of Congress and was then signed into law by Kennedy's successor, Lyndon B. Johnson.

Civil Rights Movement: The civil rights movement was a struggle for social justice that took place mainly during the 1950s and 1960s for blacks to gain equal rightsunder the law in the United States.

THE FALLACY

Collaborative Strategic Planning: Collaborative Strategic Planning (CSP), uses of eight characteristics generated through the social interaction of a selected Planning Task Force (PTF). The eight characteristics that the PTF will produce are meaningful engagement, transparency, divergence of ideas, proprietorship of the planning process and outcomes, reflective thinking and refinements, exploration and learning, an independent perspective, and connectivity with the community they serve.

Cooperative Congressional Election Study: The CCES is a 50,000+ person national stratified sample survey administered by YouGov. The survey consists of two waves in election years. In the pre-election wave, respondents answer two-thirds of the questionnaire. This segment of the survey asks about general political attitudes, various demographic factors, assessment of roll call voting choices, political information, and vote intentions.

Copyright Infringement: copyright infringement occurs when a copyrighted work is reproduced, distributed, performed, publicly displayed, or made into a derivative work without the permission of the copyright owner.

Critical Race Theory CRT: CRT is a theory that lends itself to open discussions about race and racism in American ideological society.

COVID-19 (coronavirus): a mild to severe respiratory illness that is transmitted chiefly by contact with infectious material (such as respiratory droplets) or with objects or surfaces contaminated by the causative virus, and is characterized especially by fever, cough, and shortness of breath and may progress to pneumonia and respiratory failure.

CU: Colorado University

Declaration of Independence: The public act by which the Second Continental Congress, July 4, 1776, declared the Colonies to be free and independent of England.

EDBUILD: is a nonprofit organization focused on bringing common sense and fairness to the way states fund public schools.

Emancipation Proclamation: The proclamation issued by President Lincoln on January 1, 1863 freeing the slaves in those territories still in rebellion against the Union.

ESPN: Entertainment and Sports Programming Network

Facebook: is a popular free social networking website that allows registered users to create profiles, upload photos and video, send messages and keep in touch with friends, family and colleagues.

Fair Pay to Play Act: This bill would prohibit California postsecondary educational institutions except community colleges, and every athletic association, conference, or other group or organization with authority over intercollegiate athletics, from providing a prospective intercollegiate student athlete with compensation in relation to the athlete's name, image, or likeness, or preventing a student participating in intercollegiate athletics from earning compensation as a result of the use of the student's name, image, or likeness or obtaining professional representation relating to the student's participation in intercollegiate athletics (SB 206).

FERPA: Family Educational Rights Protection Act is a Federal law that protects the privacy of student education records. The law applies to all schools that receive funds under an applicable program of the U.S. Department of Education.

FCC: Football Conference Champions

Grant-in Aid Scholarship: a federal grant is financial aid awarded to fund a specific
project or program. Recipients include state, local, and municipal governments, as well as individuals.

Hegemony/ (ic): the predominant influence exercised by a group over another.

HEI: Higher Education Institutions

Human Capital/ism: Human capitalism is defined as an investment of organizations in education and training to increase employees' knowledge, expertise, and skills, which ultimately may maximize organizational productivity and outputs.

Hysteria: as uncontrollable outbursts often characterized by irrationality.

Imbalance: An imbalance in the game of chess is any difference in two opposing positions. An imbalance is not a winning position, it is just a variation in a position. It is the responsibility of players to create an advantageous position.

Instagram: Instagram is a free, online photo-sharing application and social network platform. Instagram allows users to edit and upload photos and short videos through a mobile app. Users can add a caption to each of their posts and use hashtags and location-based to index these posts and make them searchable by other users within the app.

Jim Crow laws: Laws and policies of segregating or discriminating against African Americans.

LAPD: Los Angeles Police Department

LASD: Los Angeles Sheriff Department

Limited Liability Corporation LLC: A limited liability company (LLC) is a corporate structure in the United States whereby the owners are not personally liable for the company's debts or liabilities.

Mendez vs. Westminster: In 1946, eight years before the landmark Supreme Court decision in Brown v. Board of Education, Mexican Americans in Orange County, California won a class action lawsuit to dismantle school system segregation.

Multiculturalism: is a concept that deals with understanding and responding to challenges associated with racial diversity.

NAACP: The National Association for the Advancement of Colored People is the nation's foremost, largest, and most widely recognized civil rights organization. Its more than half-million members and supporters throughout the United States and the world are the premier advocates for civil rights in their communities, leading grassroots campaigns for equal opportunity and conducting voter mobilization.

NCES: The National Center for Education Statistics (NCES) collects, analyzes and makes available data related to education in the U.S. and other nations.

NCAA: The National Collegiate Athletic Association is a member-led organization dedicated to the well-being and lifelong success of college athletes.

NCPA: The National College Players Association (NCPA) is a 501c3 nonprofit advocacy group launched by UCLA football players that serves as the only independent voice for college athletes across the nation.

NIL: Name, Image, and Likeness

1.600 rule: The rule was devised and sanctioned to assure that all incoming freshman who participated in athletics and received a grant in aid scholarship earned a 1.600 grade point average on a 4.0 grading scale.

Planning Task Force PTF: The PTF is a group selected for their hardiness to the task of Collaborative Strategic Planning.

PSI: Post-Secondary Institutions (colleges, universities, community colleges, trade schools, etc.)

Predpol: an unreliable predictive policing software used by law enforcement.

Propaganda: as information, rumors, etc., deliberately spread widely to help or harm a person, group, movement, institution, and or nation.

Racial Capital/ ism: racial capitalism is defined as the process of deriving social or economic value from the racial identity of another.

Rhetorical behavior: refers to how the written, spoken and visual languages are used to maintain social groups, construct meanings and identities, coordinate behavior, and mediate power.

Sanity Code: In 1948, the Sanity Code was instituted by the NCAA. The Sanity Code was supposedly designed to ensure that all student athletes met all the requirements to enter college without any grant assistance.

SAT: Scholastic Aptitude Test, is an entrance exam used by most colleges and universities to make admissions decisions.

SB 206: This bill would prohibit California postsecondary educational institutions except community colleges, and every athletic association, conference, or other groups or organizations with authority over intercollegiate athletics, from providing a prospective intercollegiate student athlete with compensation in relation to the athlete's name, image, or likeness, or preventing a student participating in intercollegiate athletics from earning compensation as a result of the use of the student's name, image, or likeness or obtaining professional representation relating to the student's participation in intercollegiate athletics (Fair Pay to Play ACT).

Sherman Act: The Sherman Antitrust Act of 1890 is a federal statute which prohibits activities that restrict interstate commerce and competition in the marketplace.

SMART Goals: Smart goals and objectives are Specific, Measurable, Assignable, Realistic, and Time-related.

Strategic Planning/Management: Strategic planning/ Management is the process of documenting and establishing a direction of your small business by assessing both where you are and where you're going. The strategic plan gives you a place to record your mission, vision, and values, as well as your long-term goals and the action plans you'll use to reach them.

THE FALLACY

Student Athlete SA: "Student athlete" means an individual who engages in, is eligible to engage in or may be eligible in the future to engage in any intercollegiate sport.

TikTok: a platform to post short-form mobile video.

Title IX: a federal law that states that: No person in the United States shall, on the basis of sex, be excluded from participation, in be denied the benefits of, or besubjected to discrimination under any education program or activity receiving Federal financial
assistance.

Tokenism: The practice of making only a perfunctory or symbolic effort to do a particular thing, especially by recruiting a small number of people from underrepresented groups in order to give the appearance of sexual or racial equality within a workforce.

Trademark Infringement: is the unauthorized use of a trademark or service mark on or in connection with goods and/or services in a manner that is likely to cause confusion, deception, or mistake about the source of the goods and/or services.

Trans-Atlantic Slave Trade: a segment of the global slave trade that transported between 10 million and 12 million enslaved Africans across the Atlantic Ocean to
the Americas from the 16th to the 19th century.

Twitter: Twitter is a 'microblogging' system that allows you to send and receive short posts called tweets. Tweets can be up to 140 characters long and can include links to
relevant websites and resources.

US: United States

Worker's Compensation: Workers' compensation is a form of accident insurance paid by employers. No payroll deductions are taken out of employees' salaries for this insurance. If you're injured on the job or acquire a work-related illness, workers' comp will pay your medical expenses, and if you can't work, it will also cover wage-loss compensation until you're able to return to work.

REFERENCES

Aberson, C. L. (2007). Diversity experiences predict changes in attitudes toward affirmative action. Cultural Diversity and Ethnic Minority Psychology, 13, 285-294.

AFL-CIO America's unions (n.d.). Unions begin with you. Retrieved July 13, 2020 https://aflcio.org/what-unions-do

Ansoff, H., I. (1965). Corporate Strategy: An Analytic Approach to Business Policy for Growth and Expansion. New York: McGraw-Hill

Aschoff, E. (October 1,2019). Ohio State AD Gene Smith against Fair Pay to Play Act. Retrieved from https://www.espn.com/college-sports/story/_/id/27743871/ohio-state-ad-gene-smith-fair-pay-play-act

Barney et al, (2002). Selling The Five Rings: The International Olympic Committee and the Rise of Olympic Commercialism: Salt Lake City, The University of Utah Press

Becker, G.S. (1993), Human Capital: A Theoretical and Empirical Analysis with Special Reference to Education, 3rd ed., The University of Chicago Press, Chicago, IL.

Berkowitz, S. (2020, August, 13). College athletes 'bill of rights' unveiled by U.S. senators seeking to change NCAA systems. https://www. usatoday.com/ story/sports /college/2020/08/13/

college-sports-bill-rights-unveiled-senators-who-want-change/3362358001/

Bertrand, M., and S. Mullainathan. 2004. "Are Emily and Greg More Employable Than Lakisha and Jamal? A Field Experiment in Labor Market Discrimination." The American Economic Review 94 (4): 991–1013.

Beschloss, M. (2014). T.R.'s Son Inspired Him to Help Rescue Football. Retrieved from https://www.nytimes.com/2014/08/02/upshot/trs-son-inspired-him-to-help-rescue-football.html

Bloomberg said in 2015 'all the crime' is in minority areas. BBC News. (2020, February). Retrieved February 11, 2020, https://www.bbc.com/news/world-us-canada-51466036

Brooks, K., J. (November 1, 2019). NCAA athletes getting paid: Thousands could be in their futures. Retrieved from https://www.cbsnews.com/news/ncaa-athletes-getting-paid-thousands-could-be-in-their-future/

BUCKLAND, R. (2009) Private and Public Sector Models for Strategies in Universities*. British Journal of Management, v. 20, n. 4, p. 524-536

Burns, M., J. (March 20, 2019). Racial Divides Persist on Compensation for Student-Athletes: Blacks much more likely than whites to support compensating college athletes. Retrieved from https:// morningconsult.com /2019/03/20/racial-divides-persist-on-compensation-for-student-athletes/

Byers, W. & Hammer, C. (1995). Unsportsmanlike conduct: Exploiting college athletes. Ann Arbor: The University of Michigan Press

Clement, J. (November 21, 2019) Retrieved from
https://www.statista.com/statistics/272014 /global-social-
networks-ranked-by-number-of-users/

Cohen, A., M. & Kisker, C., B. (2nd Ed.). (2010). The Shaping of
American Higher Education: Emergence and Growth of the
Contemporary System. San Francisco, John Wiley & Sons

Crouse, L. & Stockton, A. (October 9, 2019). Everyone Made
Money Off My NCAA Career, Except Me. (Katelyn Ohashi).
Retrieved from https://www.nytimes.com/2019/10/09/
opinion/katelyn-ohashi-fair-play-act.html

Davies, R., O. (2017). Sports in American Life (3rd Ed.). West
Sussex, UK: John Wiley & Sons

Doran, G., T., (1981). There is a S.M.A.R.T. way to write
management's goals and objectives. *Management Review.*
Vol. 70 (11), p. 35-36

Dovel, G. (Nov. 9, 2019). Do the right thing, NCAA, and free
Memphis' James Wiseman. Retrieved from:
https://www.indystar.com/story/sports/columnists/gregg-
doyel/2019/11/09/ncaa-should-rule-james-wiseman-eligible-
penny-hardaway-memphis/2543926001/

Echchaibi, N. (2020, July, 10). Thou shall not erase me.
Aljazeera.https://www.aljazeera. com/indepth/opinion/thou-
erase-200707164436376.html

Elliott, M., Hughes, J. (2019). A brief History of Slavery that
You didn't learn in School. Retrieved from
https://www.nytimes.com
/interactive/2019/08/19/magazine/history-slavery-
smithsonian.html

Feagin, J. (2000). Racist America. Boston: Routledge Kegan
Paul.

#FirstTake. (September 13, 2019). Tim Tebow rails against the California amateurism law.Retrieved from https://www.youtube. com/watch ?v=KKpm4jwMi8o

Fuchs, E. (2015). JFK wrote a memo in 1961 that still has a huge impact on college admission in America. Retrieved by https://www.businessinsider.com/where-did-affirmative-action-come-from-2015-12

Glaister, D. (2004). University uproar over heiress who 'cheated'. Retrieved by https://www.theguardian.com /world/2004/nov/30/usa.internationaleducationnews

Grady, J. & Nagel, M., S. (2013). Keep Calm and Johnny Football:
The Evolving Trademark Rights of College Athletes
Sport Marketing Quarterly; 22, p. 246-248

Graham, D. (2015). Black Tape Over Black Faculty Portraits at Harvard Law School. Retrieved by https://www.theatlantic.com/politics/archive/2015/11/harvard-law-faculty-black-tape/416877/

Goldstein, J. & Southall, A. (December 6, 2019). New York Times. I Got Tired of Hunting Black and Hispanic People. Retrieved from https://www.nytimes.com/2019 /12/06/nyregion/nyc-police-subway-racial-profiling.html

Goldstein, W. (2014). Walter Camp's Off-Side: A Tarnished Football Legacy. Retrieved from https://www.courant.com/opinion/op-ed/hc-op-commentary-goldstein-yales-walter-camp-bent--20140314-story.html

Grimm, J., Grimm, W., ZIPES, J., & DEZSÖ, A. (2014). CINDERELLA. In The Original Folk and Fairy Tales of the

Brothers Grimm: The Complete First Edition (pp. 69-77). Princeton University Press. Retrieved January 20, 2020, from www.jstor.org/stable/j.ctt6wq18v.28

Hanna, J., Hartung, K., Sayers, D., M., & Almasy, S. (2017). Virginia governor to white nationalists: 'Go home ... shame on you'. Retrieved by https://www.cnn. com/2017/08/12 /us/charlottesville-white-nationalists-rally/index.html

Harris R. (2017). How much has baseball changed since the infamous Al Campanis interview? Not enough, judging by the number of African-American players and managers Retrieved from https://theundefeated.com/features/baseball-changed-since-al-campanis-interview/

Harris, T., M., Janovec, A., Murray, S., Gubbala, S. & Robinson, A. (2018). Communicating Racism: A Study of Racial Microaggressions in a Southern University and the Local Community. Southern Communication Journal, 84 (2), 72-84

Henderson, E., A. (2019). Being Black at Penn State. Retrieved by https:// www.collegian. psu.edu/opinion / letters_to_ editor/ article_56c889e0-19d6-11e9-918c-4b0acfadb892.html

Hinds, P.S., Vogel, R.J., & Clark-Steffen, L. (1997). The possibilities and pitfalls of doing a secondary analysis of qualitative data set, Qualitative Health Research, Vol. 7(3): p.408-424.

Jabbar, K., A. (January 9, 2018). It's time to pay the tab for America's college athletes. Retrieved from https://www.theguardian.com/sport/2018/jan/09/its-time-to-pay-the-tab-for-americas-college-athletes

Jackson, V., (October 11, 2018). The myth of amateurism: *How America's multi-billion-dollar college sports industry exploits its stars*. Retrieved from https://www. independent

.co.uk / sport/us-sport/college-sports-industry-exploitation-amateurism-ncaa-a8579606.html

Japan scientist 'very pessimistic' Olympics will happen next year. (2020, April 20). Retrieved from https://www. aljazeera.com/news/2020/04/japan-scientist-pessimistic-olympics-happen-year-200420093614927.html

Jennings, L., A. (June 7, 2016). For Love or For Money: A History of Amateurism in the Olympic Games Retrieved from https://www.vice.com/en_us/article/gvaqdm/for-love-or-for-money-a-history-of-amateurism-in-the-olympic-games

Karabel, J. The Chosen: The Hidden History of Admission and Exclusion at Harvard, Yale, and Princeton. Boston: Houghton Mifflin, 2005.

Ladson-Billings, G. (2000). Racialized discourses and ethnic epistemologies. In N. K. Denzin & Y.S. Lincoln (Eds.). Handbook of qualitative research (2nded., pp.257-278). Thousand Oaks, CA: Sage.

Lane, S., & Brown, A. (2016). Fallen & forgotten: Football player Rashidi Wheeler died during practice 15 years ago. But no one knows his story. Retrieved by http://apps.north bynorthwestern .com/magazine/2016/spring/features/fallen-forgotten/

Laws Mandating Data Collection Reveal Discrimination. (2020, February 10). Equal Justice Initiative. Retrieved February 10, 2020, from https://eji.org/news/laws-mandating-data-collection-reveal-discrimination/

Lennard, N. (May 19 2018). Call Congress's "Blue Lives Matter" Bills What They Are: Another Attack on Black Lives. Retrieved from https:// theintercept.com /2018/05/19/blue-lives-matter-bill-police-brutality/

Leong, N. (2013). Racial Capitalism. Harvard Law Review,

126 (8), 2151-2226

Lombardi, J. V., and others. The Sports Imperative in America's Research Universities. Tempe, Arizona: The Center for Measuring University Performance, 2003.

Lopez, G. E. (2004). Interethnic contact, curriculum and attitudes in the first year of college. Journal of Social Issues, 60, 75-94.

Loretta 8., (Jan 28, 2014). Friendly Reminder: The NCAA Invented The Term "Student-Athlete" To Get Out Of Paying Worker's Comp Retrieve from https://www.insidenu.com /2014/1/28/ 5355988/ ncaa-student-athlete-kain-colter-union-workers-comp

Mahaffy, J., (1879). Old Greek Athletics, MacMillian Magazine (36), 324-7

Mather, V. (Oct. 8, 2019). I Won Olympic Gold. Now a Word From My Sponsor. New York Times. Retrieved from https://www.nytimes.com/2019/10/08/sports/olympics/rule-40-usopc.html

McCallum, J. (September 17, 1984). Why is This Man Saying The Things He's Saying? Retrieved from https://www.si. com/ vault/1984/09/17/620487/scorecard

McCann, M. (January 16, 2020). Impact on LSU, Players If Odell Beckham Jr. Handed Out Real Money. Retrieved from https://www.si.com/college/2020/01/16/odell-beckham-jr-money-lsu-players-consequences

McDavis, C., J. (October 27, 2019). Student athletes shouldn't be paid. California's law is full of false promises. Retrieved from https://www.courant.com/opinion/op-ed/hc-op-mcdavis-student-athlete-pay-con-1027-20191027-r2fwciri4bbohmahhq4phvsxqe-story.html

Meckler, L. (2019). Report finds $23 billion racial funding gap for schools. Retrieved from https://www.washingtonpost.com/local/education/report-finds-23-billion-racial-funding-gap-for-schools/2019/02/25/d562b704-3915-11e9-a06c-3ec8ed509d15_story.html

Medium. (April 4, 2019). Stoplapdspying. Retrieved from https://medium.com/@stoplapdspying /on-tuesday-april-2nd-2019-twenty-eight-professors-and-forty-graduate-students-of-university-of-8ed7da1a8655

Metivier, S. & Barsch, J. (November 6, 2019). At the Buzzer: Jeremy Bloom talks NCAA pay for likeness, California law. Retrieved from https://www.ralphiereport.com/2019/11/6/20951678/at-the-buzzer-jeremy-bloom-talks-ncaa-pay-for-likeness-california-law

Moody, J. (2004). Faculty diversity. New York, NY: Routledge Falmer.

Morales, M., & Andone, D. (2019). Felicity Huffman gets 14 days in prison in connection with college admission scandal. Retrieved by https://www.cnn.com/2019/ 09/13/us/felicity-huffman-sentencing/index.html

Mueller (2018), "Why twitter is the ideal platform for engagement", available at: www. convinceandconvert.com/social-media-strategy/twitter-engagement/(accessed21October2018)

Murphy, D. (2020, April 28). Source: NCAA group to propose possible changes to allow athlete endorsements. https://www.espn.com/college-sports/story/_/id/29109389

Nazarvan, A. (April 21, 2016). Lie and Deny: Secrecy and Suspicion Surround the Los Angeles County Sheriff's

Department Retrieved from https://www.newsweek.com /los-angeles-county-sheriffs-department-mitrice-richardson-secrecy-suspicion-450421

NCAA 2018-2019 Division 1 Manual. (2018, August). Retrieved from https://web3. ncaa.org/lsdbi/reports/getReport/90008

Nieto, S. (1992). Affirming diversity: The sociopolitical context of multicultural education. New York, NY: Longman. New York Times. September 8, 2002. Retrieved from: https://www.nytimes.com / 2014/08/02/ upshot/trs-son-inspired-him-to-help-rescue-football.html

Nocera, J., & Strauss, B. (2018). Indentured: The Battle to end the Exploitation of College Athletes. New York: Portfolio/Penguin

NPR. (April 21, 2014). Hunger Games: College Athletes Make Play For Collective Bargaining Retrieved from https://www.npr .org/ sections/ thesalt/2014/ 04 /21/ 304196202/hunger-games-college-athletes-make-play-for-collective-bargaining

O'Bannon, E., McCann, M. (2018). Court Justice: The inside story of my battle against the NCAA. Diversion Books

Omi, M., &Winant, H. (1994). Racial formation in the United States: Fromthe1960stothe 1990s (2nd ed.). Boston: Routledge Kegan Paul.

Popay, J., Rogers, A., & Williams, G. (1998). Rationale and standards for the systematic review of qualitative literature in health services research, Qualitative Health Research. Vol. 8 (3). p. 329-340

Poston, B., & Chang, C. (2019,). LAPD searches blacks and Latinos more. But they're less likely to have contraband than whites. Retrieve from https://www.latimes.com /local/lanow/la-me-lapd-searches-20190605-story.html

Puente, M. & Chang, C. (October 16, 2019,). LAPD will adjust data-driven predictor. Los Angeles Times, B3

Ramsay, G. (2020, March, 24). Japanese PM and IOC chief agree to postpone 2020 Olympics until 2021. retrieved by https://edition.cnn.com/2020/03/24/sport/olympics-postponement-tokyo-2020-spt-intl/index.html.

Rattansi, S. (2020, August 10). US police's facial recognition systems misidentify Black people [Video]. https://www.aljazeera.com/news/2020/08/polices-facial-recognition-systems-misidentify-black-people-200810140251252.html

Raphael, J., T. (2012). Next Steps in Social Media: Turning followers into customers. Audience Development, p. 22-26

Rizatti, G.; Rizatti, Jr., G. (2005). Importância do Planejamento para as Universidades. Anais Colóquio Internacional sobre Gestão Universitária na América do Sul, Florianópolis, SC, Brasil, 5

Sage G. H., (1998). Power and Ideology in American Sport: A Critical Perspective: Second Edition. Champaign, IL. Human Kinetics

Sanaghan, P. (2009). Collaborative Strategic Planning in Higher Education. NACUBO. Washington, D.C.

Siegel, B. (2020, June, 9). Why protesters want to defund the police after George Floyd's death. ABCNews.

FALLACY

https://www.goodmorningamerica. com/news/ story/
protesters-defund-police-george-floyds-death-71123610

Silman, J. (1993). (3rd.Ed). How to Reassess Your Chess: The
complete chess mastery course. Los Angeles, Siles Press.

Slear, T., (2019/2020, Winter). Underdog No More.
Splash, 33-35.

Sport Business (June 26, 2019). IOC approves 'evolution' of
Olympic Games bidding. Retrieved from
https://www.sportbusiness.com/news/ioc-approves-
evolution-of-olympic-games-bidding/

Stoldt, G. C. & Vermillion, M. (2013). The organizational roles
of college athletics communicators: Relationship to the use
and perceptions of social media. International Journal of
Sport Communication, 6, 185-202

Tate, W. F., IV. (1997). Critical race theory and education:
History, theory and implications. In M. Apple (Ed.), Review of
research in education (pp. 191-243). Washington, DC:
American Educational Research Association.

Team USA (2020). Athlete Services. (Teamusa.org). Retrieved
from https://www.teamusa.org /team-usa-athlete-services
/athlete-marketing/ioc-rule-40-ipc-athlete-image-policy-
guidelines

Thamel, O. (January 31, 2017,). The stream team.
Sport Illustrated, 126(4), 62-66

Vu, N. (2019). These Harvard Law Students Said The School
Didn't Do Enough After They Were Targeted With Racist And
Sexist Messages. Retrieved by https://www.buzzfeednews.
com / article/nancyvu/these-harvard-law-students-say-the-
school-didnt-do-enough

Walker, L., Baines, P., Dimitriu, R. and Macdonald, E. (2017), "Antecedents of retweeting in a (political) marketing context", Psychology and Marketing, 34 (3) p.275.

Wagner, J. & Belson, K. (2020, April 28). Some Sports May Have to Skip This Year, Fauci Says. https://www. nytimes .com/2020/04/28/sports/fauci-sports-reopening-pandemic.html

Webster's Encyclopedia Unbridged Dictionary of the English Language (1989). Gramercy Publishing.

Weissman, J. (2019). 43 Percent of White Students Harvard Admits Are Legacies, Jocks, or the Kids of Donors and Faculty. Retrieved from https:// slate.com/ business/ 2019/09/ harvard-admissions -affirmative-action-white-students-legacy-athletes-donors.html

Wharton, D. (Oct. 8, 2019). Olympic athletes earn the right to market themselves during 2020 Games. Los Angeles Times. Retrieved from https://www.latimes .com / sports /olympics/story /2019-10-08/olympic-athletes-tokyo-2020-games

Winston, A. & Burrington (April 26, 2018). verge.com. A pioneer in predictive policing is starting a troubling new project. Retrieved from https://www.theverge.com/2018 /4/26/17285058/ predictive-policing-predpol-pentagon-ai-racial-bias

Womack, A. & Morgan, J. (1995). Market value: Variables determining faculty salaries. Black Issues In Higher Education, 12,12-15

.

FALLACY

AUTHOR'S PAGE

Mark Adkins is a devoted husband, father of two, and part-time author at large. He enjoys sketching, painting, as well as, spending time riding the waves and eating tacos at the beach.

If you would like to leave a review, comment, and or question for either of Mark's books, please log on to **www.easywritor.com**. Also, at **easywritor.com** you can find about his latest projects and favorite tacos dives.

The proceeds from the books go directly to Mark's pursuit of a Doctorate of Philosophy (PhD.). Graduate school is expensive. So, if you can be a gifter, buy three, keep one and give two away as gifts. Mahalo!